The Narrow Gate

Kristoffer Paulsson

The Narrow Gate

info@thotlm.org
https://thotlm.org
First edition

ISBN 978-91-984752-3-4

Contents

Preface vii

Introduction xix

1 Repent and Turn From Sin 3

2 Confession of Sin 11

3 The Condition of Man 17

4 The Inability of Man 23

5 God Seeks the Lost 29

6 Final Judgement 33

7 Lost Forever 39

8 The Law and Sin 45

9 First Commandment 51

10 Second Commandment 59

11 Third Commandment 65

12 Fourth Commandment 71

13 Fifth Commandment 77

14 Sixth Commandment 81

15 Seventh Commandment 85

16 Eighth Commandment 89

17 Ninth Commandment 93

18 Tenth Commandment 99

19 Salvation 107

20 Transition to Light 113

21 Receive Salvation 119

22 Fulfill Salvation 125

23 Born Again 131

24 The Narrow Gate 139

25 The Narrow (and Holy) Way 145

26 Faith in Jesus 153

27 Faith Comes by Hearing 161

28 The Cross 167

29 Justification 173

30 Reconciliation With God 179

31 Pure Conscience and Heart 185

Conclusion 193

Preface

The Good News of Salvation

Sin

> [12] So then, just as sin entered the world through one man and death through sin, and so death spread to all people because all sinned–
>
> — Romans 5:12

In the beginning, God created the world, Adam and Eve; everything was perfect. There was no evil or death in the creation. God created humanity with a free will; he also created the tree of life and the tree of knowledge of good and evil. There was a choice man could make, to walk with God and live or to walk his own way, without God.

When Adam ate of the fruit from the tree of knowledge, he gained knowledge about right and wrong. Then, the man could choose if he wanted to do good or evil, but at the same time, he rejected God.

When humanity rejected God, we separated from the source of life with the result of death, sin, and evil that came into the world. This means that all people are dead, separated from God so that we can no longer fellowship with him anymore. Since then, man has lost the meaning of life.

Humanity has since then tried to get back to God through religion. Always based on the same idea, that we are supposed to become better humans to appease God. If humanity has been in denial of God's existence, he has always tried to do something about his condition through ideology or philosophy.

Fact is, humanity is eternally separated from God, there is nothing it can do to compensate for its wickedness. Humanity is fallen!

The Law

> [20] For no one is declared righteous before him by the works of the law, for through the law comes the knowledge of sin
>
> — Romans 3:20

When God delivered the people of Israel from the slavery in Egypt through Moses, he took them through the

wilderness to the land of Canaan. In the wilderness, God gave the Israelites the law, and in the Law, the Ten Commandments of God.

It's easy for a person to look at their environment and think that they are good. Often we think: "I'm not worse than the others. I'm even better than he or she." Then we usually believe that we are good enough to be accepted by God.

Let's examine this by looking at three out of ten commandments: number six, seven and eight:

6 § *You shall not commit adultery.*

In Matthew 5:28, Jesus says that a man who looks at a woman with lust commits adultery with her in his heart. This also applies in reverse. The question is then: Have you ever been looking at another person (opposite or same sex) with sexual desire, ever in your whole life? It's enough that you've done it once to be counted for sin!

7 § *You shall not steal.*

In the seventh commandment: You shall not steal. What does it mean to steal? Test yourself according to this: Have you ever robbed the bank? Have you ever stolen anything? Have you snatched? Have you taken something from another person? Even when you were a kid? It does not matter how large or small the crime is!

8 § *You shall not bear false witness against your neighbor.*

So what does it mean to bear false witness? One could ask themselves. Have you ever lied in court under oath? Ever accused someone, when you were mistaken? Have you ever talked trash about someone? Or simply just gossiped? You know yourself if you are guilty or not.

Guilty or not guilty? Now we have reviewed only three of the ten commandments. According to Jewish tradition, there is a total of 613 bids in the Law of Moses, while the New Testament contains more than 1000 regulations of what God expects of us. No human being has ever managed to match the demands that God requires of us for righteousness. Therefore we are all guilty of sin.

The Sacrificial Service

> [6] So with these things prepared like this,
> the priests enter continually into the outer
> tent as they perform their duties. [7] But
> only the high priest enters once a year into
> the inner tent, and not without blood that
> he offers for himself and for the sins of
> the people committed in ignorance.
>
> — Hebrews 9:6-7

In the Old Testament, we have the sacrificial system and the temple service. The reason why it was necessary to sacrifice was to divert the wrath of God for the sins of the people. The Bible clearly states that the wages of sin are death (Romans 6:23).

Shouldn't God be angry for all the evil committed on

the earth? War, murder, rape, theft. Yes, all acts that cause harm towards one and another. Therefore God must be angry at the sin committed by us, not just about specific sins but all sin!

Because of the wrath of God over sin, bloodshed is required, so that justice is rendered. In the temple, sinners sacrificed a lamb, sheep, ram or bull to derive the wrath of God that was upon them. The priest and the sinner put their hands on the head of the beast, confessed the sins and thereby transferred the sins on to the creature to be sacrificed. Then the animal was sacrificed on behalf of the sinner.

This sacrifice is a ritual accomplished in the place for the sinner. This derived God's wrath from the sinner so that he wouldn't have to die in his transgressions. The temple service in the Old Testament covered the sinner for a period of up to a year.

Eternal Punishment

> 7 Do not be deceived. God will not be made
> a fool. For a person will reap what he sows,
> 8 because the person who sows to his own

> flesh will reap corruption from the flesh,
> but the one who sows to the Spirit will
> reap eternal life from the Spirit.
>
> — Galatians 6:7-8

For those who have sinned, even if it is a minor sin, the wrath of God is upon them too. This is called in the Bible to be in debt or to bear iniquity.

Every person will one day have to answer to the creator for everything they have done in their life. It's enough to commit one sin to be guilty. If you are guilty, you will spend the eternity after this life separated from God.

The place where the sinner will spend eternity is called hell and is a place of fire and sulfur. Once you go there, there is no chance to escape, and the punishment is forever.

The Cross

> [16] and to reconcile them both in one body to God through the cross, by which the hostility has been killed.
>
> — Ephesians 2:16

Jesus is the sacrificial Lamb of God! Two thousand years ago God sent his only begotten Son, Jesus Christ. He was born by a virgin and placed under the Law, while at the same time being God. He walked here among us and experienced what it is like to be human. He experienced evil, temptation and everything that comes against all of us.

But Jesus was born without original sin and walked on the Earth without ever falling into sin. By doing so, he managed to keep the whole law that no other man ever did, while being able to have compassion for us dead humans.

Not only is Jesus the Son of God, but he is also the sacrificial Lamb of God. When Jesus was crucified on the Cross of Calvary he died and resurrected from the dead, for us. Jesus is the sacrificial lamb who paid the price of all sin, guilt, and shame. His sacrificial death does not only cover us but also washes us wholly white and clean.

Grace

> [15] But the gracious gift is not like the transgression. For if the many died through the transgression of the one man, how much more did the Grace of God and the gift by the grace of the one man Jesus Christ multiply to the many!
>
> — Romans 5:15

Jesus came to us to be among us and pay the price for our guilt. This is the Grace of God upon humanity. Grace does not mean that we can use Jesus' sacrificial death as an apology for our sinful lifestyle but is the power of God unto salvation.

Through the Cross, God gave us his mercy to be the children of God and to have all our debt paid. In our place, God punished his own Son because of the wrath for the sin of the world.

To overcome the sin and escape the eternal

punishment, we must make use of the grace, which God has given us through his only begotten Son on the Cross of Calvary.

The grace that God has given us does not apply automatically. To take part in grace, we must receive salvation from God's extended hand. An active response from our side is needed to receive God's gift.

Jesus as Lord

> [16] Therefore let us confidently approach the throne of grace to receive mercy and find grace whenever we need help.
>
> — Hebrews 4:16

To receive salvation, we must:

- Repent from our evil ways
- Confess our sin
- Ask for forgiveness
- Claim that Jesus is the sacrifice for our sins

- Believe that Jesus is God's only begotten Son and that he is alive today.
- Make Jesus Lord in our lives and proclaim it publicly.

We get delivered from:

- Sin
- Debt
- Shame
- Disease
- Shackles
- Iniquity

We get:

- A pure heart
- Peace with God
- Hope about eternity
- Adopted as children of God

If we persevere, we will get an everlasting life and rise from the dead.

Introduction

The Faith

& Walk With Jesus

Welcome to an introduction on the faith and walk with Jesus. This book was initially a blog used for evangelization. The blog has been reworked into this book. The best posts have been adapted as chapters, a total of 31. The setup of this book is to explain the Law and the Gospel, in a traditional evangelistic style. Each chapter will walk you through one topic at a time. Hopefully, this will give you a deeper insight into the gospel, and how you can come to Jesus for salvation. But not only how to come to Jesus, but also some basics on how to walk with him on the road. This teaching is aimed primarily at seekers and everyday Christians, but those who are seasoned in the walk with Jesus might find some good advice.

The blog was originally written in Swedish and been translated into English. Initially, the author consequently used the SFB15 bible-translation. While translating this book, the author wanted to use modern English, at the same time being faithful to the original meaning. Therefore more than one bible-translation has been used in English, which best fits the original text. Among others New English Translation (NET©), Complete Jewish Bible (CJB) and the King James Version (KJV). Some ancient wordings in the KJV is updated with their modern counterpart. For example "thou" with "you" and "brethren" with "brothers."

The message of the book can be split into four sections. Make Jesus Lord in our lives and proclaim it publicly.

Sin and Judgment

The first chapters deals with the human condition and inability, the consequence of living in sin and repentance.

- Repent and Turn from Sin
- Confession of Sin
- The Condition of Man
- The Inability of Man
- God Seeks the Lost
- Final Judgment
- Lost Forever

The Law and Commandments

Next, the reader has the opportunity to get acquainted with their self-righteousness. We explain sin as well as the law. As well as provide the opportunity for self-reflection in the light of the Ten Commandments of God.

- The Law and Sin

- First Commandment
- Second Commandment
- Third Commandment
- Fourth Commandment
- Fifth Commandment
- Sixth Commandment
- Seventh Commandment
- Eighth Commandment
- Ninth Commandment
- Tenth Commandment

Salvation

How do you get saved? We are trying to provide answers to this. The new birth, the Narrow Gate, and the Narrow Road are essential concepts described in these chapters.

- Salvation
- Transition to Light
- Receive Salvation
- Fulfill Salvation

- Born Again
- The Narrow Gate
- The Narrow (and Holy) Way

Faith

What does it mean to believe, and how will it affect me? We review what faith means, the Cross, justification, and other things.

- Faith in Jesus
- Faith Comes by Hearing
- The Cross
- Justification
- Reconciliation with God
- Pure Conscience and Heart

Once you have read and studied this material, we hope that you have a more solid foundation in your faith and a deeper understanding of your journey.

Chapter I

Repent and Turn From Sin

To repent of sin is not the same as saying oops and then excuse yourself. It is much deeper and goes much further down in the heart.

Conviction

> [8] And when he comes, he will **prove** the world wrong concerning sin and righteousness and judgment–
>
> — John 16:8

Jesus sent his successor, the Holy Spirit, to us to convict the world of sin. Many people have mistaken conviction for judging, but those two are different things.

When the conviction of the Holy Spirit comes, it is easy to be angry and resentful. The reason for this is that we confuse it with judgment and condemnation. Satan loves to mess around with our emotions when the Holy Spirit is trying to help us. Satan will try to push feelings of condemnation on us. Don't fall for this trick; it will alienate you from God.

When the Holy Spirit convicts you of sin, he gives you a supernatural understanding that you have sinned; why it is a sin, and that God has been grieved by your sin, that you have committed evil against someone else, and that you are feeling bad because of it. Your conscience will always knock on the door, trying to urge you to repent from your sin.

A Gift From God

> 4 Or do you have contempt for the wealth of his kindness, forbearance, and patience, and yet do not know that God's kindness

> leads you to **repentance**?
>
> — Romans 2:4

True repentance is a gift from God. It is something that God, through the Holy Spirit, works in us when he wants to point out our committed sins, which he wants us to repent from, so that we can escape the condemnation, because of our iniquity. It is critical that we do not resist the conviction of the Holy Spirit when it comes. If we do that, we harden our hearts.

Below is a bible-text explaining how true repentance from God works.

Divine Sorrow Unto Salvation – 2 Corinthians 7:8-10

> 8 For even if I made you sad by my letter, I
> do not regret having written it even though
> I did regret it, for I see that my letter made
> you sad, though only for a short time.
> 9 Now I rejoice, not because you were made
> sad, *but because you were made sad to
> the point of repentance. For you were made
> sad as God intended*, so that you were not
> harmed in any way by us.

> [10] *For* ***sadness*** *as intended by God produces a* ***repentance*** *that leads to* ***salvation****, leaving no regret*, but worldly sadness brings about death.

The divine sorrow from God, which tries to touch our hearts deeply, is God pouring repentance into our hearts so that we can repent. This gives us deep anguish, and if it is allowed to continue, it brings us unto salvation from sin.

Sorrow of the World

> [24] Then Saul said to Samuel, "I have sinned, for I have disobeyed what the LORD commanded and what you said as well. For I was afraid of the army, and I followed their wishes. [25] Now please forgive my sin! Go back with me so I can worship the LORD."
>
> — 1 Samuel 15:24-25

There is a story in the Bible, where King Saul would attack and take revenge on his enemies. The prophet Samuel had given strict orders on how this should be carried out. Saul did not obey the instructions; instead, he did it his way. This had happened several times before, while Saul was king. Finally, God spoke through the prophet Samuel that God rejected Saul because he had rejected the word of God. The feeling in the verses above is the reaction of Saul. Saul becomes pitiful because of the consequences and blames the people for breaking the instructions while hoping for light-hearted forgiveness. God chooses to reject Saul because his repentance is not sincere. The remorse of the world leads to death.

A Sorrow From God

> [6] Against you, you only, have I sinned and done what is evil from your perspective; so that you are right in accusing me and justified in passing sentence. ...[19] My sacrifice to God is a broken spirit; God, you won't spurn a broken, chastened heart.
>
> — Psalm 51:6, 19 (CJB)

We can read about King David in the Bible, how he falls in love with another man's wife and commits adultery with her. She becomes pregnant. To cover this up, David plans and assassinates her husband, Uriah. God sees all of this and sends the prophet Nathan to confront King David. Instead of blame-shifting, David understands that he has sinned against God and chose to repent. God gives him a broken heart with sincere remorse through which God can forgive King David. According to the Law of Moses, King David was up for the death penalty.

Sorrow: If we allow the Holy Spirit to do his work in us, after that we have been convicted of sin, and without resisting him or denying our condition. Then God lets sorrow be poured into our hearts so that we can mourn over our sin. If we can not grieve over our sin and condition, then it's over with us.

Regret: If we allow the divine sorrow to work in our heart according to the will of God, then it leads to genuine, profound brokenness of our evil behavior. That is remorse and regret that is sincere before God.

Salvation: When we have sincere remorse in our heart before God, then the power of the Cross can work in our lives, and our heart can be washed clean, our debts can be extinct, and the mystery of Christ will save us from sin. In this mystery of Christ, we get a new heart created in us that is pure and upright before God. This is where we receive righteousness as a gift from God when the blood of Jesus has purified us through sincere repentance.

Chapter 2

Confession of Sin

One of the most important things you need to do, to be forgiven by God is to confess your sin. Not confessing your sin is the same as not acknowledging that you have failed, which is necessary to be forgiven and cleansed by God.

Read the bible-text that describes how confession and forgiveness relate to each other.

Purification by Confession - 1 John 1:5-10

5 Now this is the gospel message we have

> heard from him and announce to you: God
> is light, and in him there is no darkness at
> all.
> 6 If we say we have fellowship with him
> and yet keep on walking in the darkness,
> we are lying and not practicing the truth.
> 7 But if we walk in the light as he himself
> is in the light, we have fellowship with one
> another and the blood of Jesus his Son
> cleanses us from all sin.
> 8 *If we say we do not bear the guilt of sin,*
> *we are deceiving ourselves and the truth is*
> *not in us.*
> 9 But if we **confess** our sins, he is faithful
> and righteous, **forgiving** us our sins and
> cleansing us from all unrighteousness.
> 10 If we say we have not sinned, we make
> him a liar and his word is not in us.

Sin is more complicated than we generally understand. It can be in several different modes in our heart. Unconscious sin. That is trespasses that we do not know about. Conscious but secret sin. The sin that we know about, but have not confessed. Revealed and confessed sin. The sin that we were aware of and now have confessed.

Unaware Sin

> [12] So then, just as sin entered the world
> through one man and death through sin,
> and so death spread to all people because
> all sinned– [13] for before the law was given,
> sin was in the world, *but there is no*
> ***accounting*** *for sin when there is no* ***law***.
>
> — Romans 5:12-13

A person who has no concept of what righteousness is has no idea that they are sinning. They live their lives as if everything was fine and hopes for the best in the end. The Bible says that where there is no law, there is no sin. No law, no accountability!

But because all are descendants of Adam, all have died a spiritual death, and have lost all hope of eternity. The sins are unknown to the individual. To have a chance to deal with their sin, they must become aware. **Here they are dead before God**.

Secret Sin

> [20] For no one is declared righteous before him by the works of the law, for through the law comes the **knowledge** of sin....[23] for all have sinned and fall short of the glory of God.
>
> — Romans 3:20, 23

God gave his law through Moses to Israel. The purpose of the Law is to teach humanity about sin, righteousness, and judgment. No one becomes righteous by keeping the Law in their own strength. The Law can be seen as a ruler, by applying the Law, it reveals the distance between the righteousness of God and the condition of man. The gap in between is called self-righteousness and constitutes the definition of sin. Now sin has been revealed to them, and they understand their guilt. **Here they are judged before God**.

Forgiven Sin

> [16] *So **confess** your sins to one another and*

> *pray for one another so that you may be* ***healed***. The prayer of a righteous person has great effectiveness.
>
> — James 5:16

To have the forgiveness at work in your life; it is vital that the sin you are aware of in your life, is revealed and becomes known to you as sin. If you realize that you have sin in your life; and you have light about it, but keep it a secret, you are wandering in darkness and remain judged by the Law. Thereby you are without the grace of God.

If you confess your sin, in the light of Jesus, by confessing your sins to one another (to someone trustworthy), God is faithful and forgives you your sin and cleanses you. **Here they stand righteous before God**.

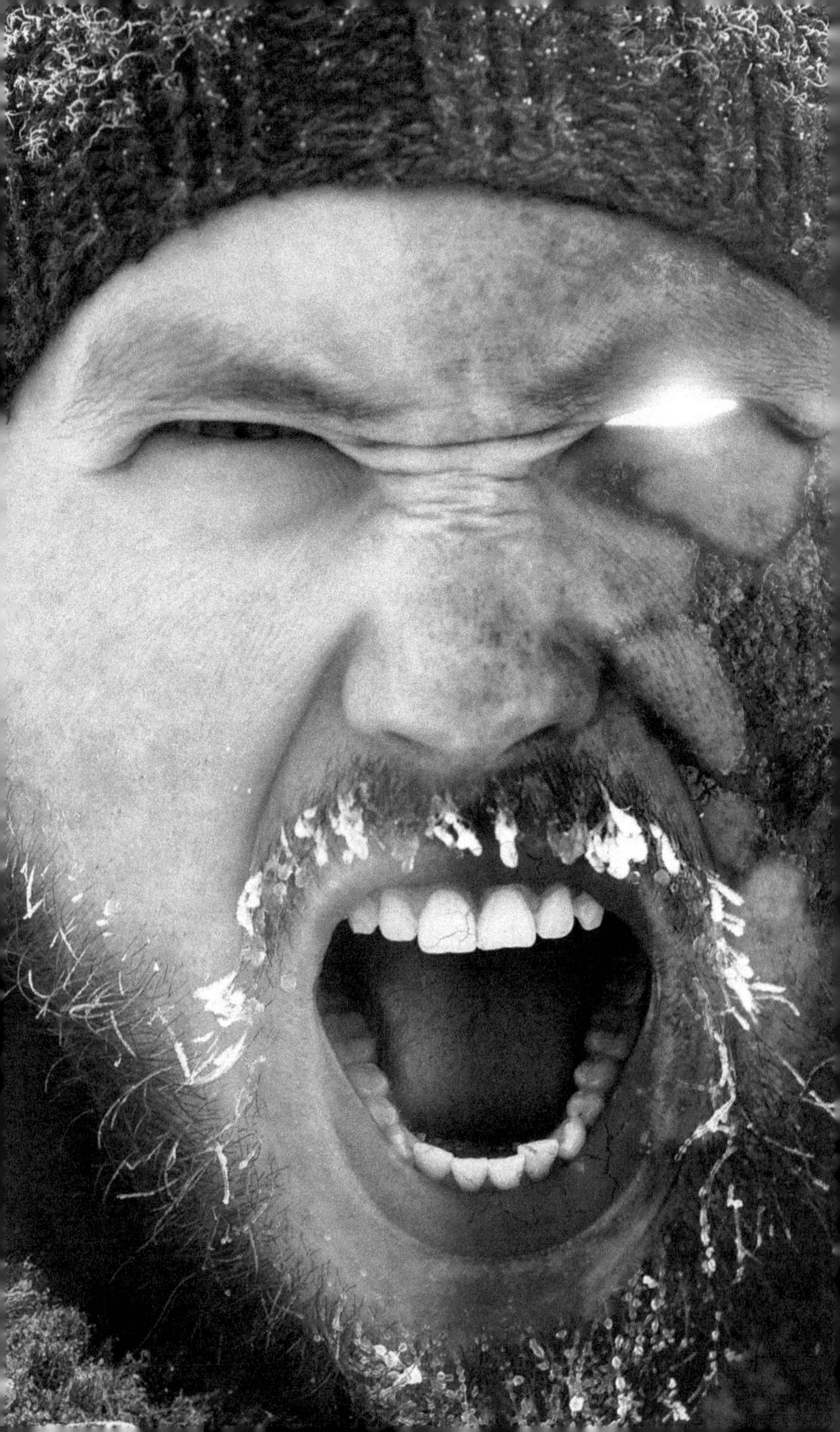

Chapter 3

The Condition of Man

Everyone is Dead Through Sin

What is our condition? Are we as good, sweet and perfect as we think we are?

> [12] So then, just as sin entered the world
> through one man and death through sin,
> and so death spread to all people because
> all sinned–
>
> — Romans 5:12

Humankind was initially created good and alive.

Spiritually alive so that we had a relationship with God. With the fall of sin at the beginning of creation, humanity died spiritually, and we were cut off from God. Through the sin of Adam, against God, death came into the world. Death separated us from God, and all descendants of Adam have part of this as their inheritance. Hence everyone is wicked doing evil, which is part of our nature: the fallen nature of Adam, also known as original sin.

The Wicked Heart

> [17:9] The human mind is more deceitful than anything else. It is incurably bad. Who can understand it?...[15:19] For out of the heart come evil ideas, murder, adultery, sexual immorality, theft, false testimony, slander.
>
> — Jeremiah 17:9, Matthew 15:19

It is in the heart that we have our thoughts, feelings, and emotions, it is there we make our plans and decisions. All the evil we see in the earth today; war, misery, violence, and oppression is rooted in the heart of humanity. Someone had an evil desire and set up a plan accordingly; someone else made a choice to act selfishly at the expense of others. All of this is unrighteousness, and it all originates from the chronically ill heart of us humans.

Slave to Sin

> 34 Jesus answered them, "I tell you the solemn truth, everyone who practices sin is a slave of sin.
>
> — John 8:34

Everyone has sinned because of the nature that we inherited from Adam. Through the evil of our hearts, we practice sin against each other in all our ways, habits and actions. Because of that, we are sold as slaves to sin. Sin is such a burden that we are incapable of changing it. We can only go in one direction, and that is what the nature of sin desires of us: wickedness!

Children of Wrath

> 3 among whom all of us also formerly lived

> out our lives in the cravings of our flesh, indulging the desires of the flesh and the mind, and were by nature children of wrath even as the rest...
>
> — Ephesians 2:3

Because we are evil and practice sin, there is a wrath of God over that sin. This anger is aimed at the practitioners of evil, the whole humanity on an individual basis. All of us are under judgment and will receive our fair share of the wrath of God at judgment day, coming at the end of this age. Everyone is therefore under the wrath of God.

Total Depravity

> [10] just as it is written: "*There is no one righteous, not even one,* [11] *there is no one who understands, there is no one who seeks God.* [12] *All have **turned away**, together they **have become worthless**; there is no one who shows kindness, not even one.*"
>
> — Romans 3:10-12

No one is righteous, everyone has the nature of sin, and everyone has sinned at least once, following their selfish desires. No one gets away with it, the whole of humankind, every individual has fallen away from God. Everyone is by nature entirely corrupted, and can not do anything about it. That is total depravity!

Chapter 4

The Inability of Man

The condition of humanity is that we are entirely depraved, because of our fallen nature from Adam. Is there anything we can do about it. Can we fix it?

Unable to Follow God

> [7] because the outlook of the flesh is hostile to God, for it does not submit to the law of God, nor is it able to do so. [8] Those who are in the flesh cannot please God.
>
> — Romans 8:7-8

Since the fall of sin, humanity is automatically hostile to God because of our fallen nature. We are automatically hostile toward God, and to walk in fellowship with him. If we learn the law and moral of God; then we will automatically do what is against God. We do what is wrong because it is part of us, a built-in rebellion. There is no chance that we can follow God, even if we try to do so. The old Adam within us will do the opposite, and we will follow the fallen nature instinctively.

Unable to Change

> [18] A good tree is not able to bear bad fruit, nor a bad tree to bear good fruit. [19] Every tree that does not bear good fruit is cut down and thrown into the fire.
>
> — Matthew 7:18-19

By ourselves, we are unable to change. Just in the same way that a pear tree cannot carry apples, nor an apple tree can carry pears. No matter how much they wish to, just as little, can a bad tree bear good fruit! Similarly, we can not change ourselves to start doing the good acts by ourselves. There is nothing about us in our DNA, that can turn us into something good.

Unable to Recompense

> [6] We are all like one who is unclean, all our so-called righteous acts are like a menstrual rag in your sight. We all wither like a leaf; our sins carry us away like the wind.
>
> — Isaiah 64:6

If we would get the opportunity to repay for all our evil, we are not able to do so. If it ever were possible for us to compensate for lousy karma by doing good deeds that produced good karma, it would just be a zero game. If ever possible! Our "good" deeds are like a dirty cloth; it's self-righteousness. Because of our sin, we carry on iniquity, something we will never be able to compensate. What does it matter if you can balance an overdraft credit but had another bank loan of ten million? You would already be bankrupt. In the same way, we are spiritually bankrupt before God.

Unable to Do Right

> [18] For I know that nothing good lives in me, that is, in my flesh. For I want to do the good, but I cannot do it.
>
> — Romans 7:18

But if I want to do what is right and just do ...then you will soon notice that you are not able to. There is a dark shadow in you that lives its own life within. To which whom you are a slave and which will never submit to God and his righteousness. All of us are born as slaves to sin.

Only the Mercy of Jesus

> [27] All things have been handed over to me by my Father. No one knows the Son except the Father, *and no one knows the Father except the Son and anyone to whom the Son decides to* ***reveal*** *him.*
>
> — Matthew 11:27

The Father has delegated everything to the Son. The

Son knows the Father and the Father knows the Son. If Jesus wants to, he can reveal the Father to you, but everything depends on the mercy of God. Only by the initiative of God, you can receive mercy. Under no circumstances can you achieve or deserve this, there is nothing you can do to fix this. Only according to the way God offers it to you, you can have mercy and salvation. In no way can you save yourself or get salvation by going your own way!

Chapter 5

God Seeks the Lost

If we who are mortal human beings, are entirely depraved and there is nothing we can do about that. What hope do we have?

> [32] And I (Jesus), when I am lifted up from the earth, *will draw all people to myself*.
>
> — John 12:32

Jesus says in the Bible that he draws all people to himself. There is no one among those who have heard about Jesus that does not have an opinion about him. Of those who have not heard of him, he raises the deep questions about:

- Who am I?
- What is the meaning of life?
- Where do we come from?
- Where do I go when I die?

The people that Jesus draws close to him, even if they don't know who he is, will do whatever they can to find the truth.

> [44] No one can come to me unless the Father who sent me **draws** him, and I will raise him up at the last day. [45] It is written in the prophets, "And they will all be taught by God." Everyone who **hears** and **learns** from the Father comes to me.
>
> — John 6:44-45

Deep down in the heart of every person, a silent and quiet voice whispers hoping that you will listen to it. That voice wants to make sure that you discover the truth about the meaning of life and where you are heading. That voice hopes you will listen and find out who he is that is talking to you and draws you. It is God who seeks you and who wants you to learn and find the way. Those who listen and learns will find the way.

> [7] So God again ordains a certain day,
> "Today," speaking through David after so
> long a time, as in the words quoted before,
> "O, that today you would listen as he
> speaks! Do not harden your hearts."
>
> — Hebrews 4:7

It's incredibly easy to silence that little voice. You may want to stay unaware of where you are heading or that there is an eternity waiting for you. Perhaps you chase the good life and think that temporary pleasure is the most important thing in this life. But do not let anything stop you from finding the truth, do not put the lid on, even if it feels uncomfortable. Be prepared to follow the voice wherever it leads you. Also, be sure to have a love for the truth even if it is unpleasant.

> [20] Listen! I am standing at the door and
> knocking! If anyone hears my voice and
> opens the door I will come into his home
> and share a meal with him, and he with me.
>
> — Revelation 3:20

God is seeking to have a private and personal relationship with you. This will set you apart from the rest of the world and comes at a price, but glory is forever!

Chapter 6

Final Judgement

Judge or not to judge, that's the question! Is it necessary that God is a judge? Some people find it hard that God is a judge, while others can't understand why there is evil in the world if God is so good.

How can a God that is good, judge people? The answer to that question is; that a judge who acquits a bank robber or a murderer is an unjust judge. Similarly, if God were to judge all people directly, no one would survive. God is patiently waiting for you to turn from your sin.

Everybody Will be Judged

> [27] *And just as people are appointed to die once, and then to face* ***judgment****,*
>
> — Hebrews 9:27

Once we have lived our lives here on earth, we will all stand before God for the final judgment by him. On that day everyone will be tried, not just for what we did but also for what we thought in our hearts.

Final Judgment - Revelation 20:11-12

> [11] Then I saw a large white throne and the one who was seated on it; the earth and the heaven fled from his presence, and no place was found for them.
> [12] And I saw the dead, the great and the small, standing before the throne. Then books were opened, and another book was opened– the book of life. So the dead were judged by what was written in the books, according to their deeds.

By the end of ages, when the earth and heaven have

completed their courses, everyone, dead and alive will be judged for their actions. In heaven, the angels keep track of everything we do and write it down to make sure we get a fair judgment, on the last and final day.

It is essential to understand the difference between a penalty and to be sentenced. Some sins are worse than others, but regardless of whether the sins are great or small, few or many, we will not be pardoned. Whoever is guilty in the court of God does not have their names in the book of life.

Sowing and Reaping

> 7 Do not be deceived. God will not be made
> a fool. For a person will reap what he sows,
> 8 because the person who sows to his own
> flesh will reap corruption from the flesh,
> but the one who sows to the Spirit will
> reap eternal life from the Spirit.
>
> — Galatians 6:7-8

Already after the flood, God taught humanity the law of sowing and reaping. He who sows injustice by breaking the Law of God, will reap a judgment at the end of time and then get a fair punishment for their sins.

God's Righteous Judgment - Romans 2:5-8

> 5 But because of your stubbornness and your unrepentant heart, you are storing up wrath for yourselves in the day of wrath, when God's righteous judgment is revealed!
> 6 He will reward each one according to his works:
> 7 eternal life to those who by perseverance in good works seek glory and honor and immortality,
> 8 but wrath and anger to those who live in selfish ambition and do not obey the truth but follow unrighteousness.

Even if you have done good things in your life, you cannot compensate your offenses with good works; what you have done you have no power to get undone. It is like sowing both wheat and thistles in the same field. When the miller is about to make flour of the grain, it must not be a mixed compote with weed. You want to have pure powder in the sack, that means:

don't think you can cheat!

Chapter 7

Lost Forever

What happens when we die? Do our Soul and Spirit continue to stay conscious without the body?

Fear God

> [28] Do not be afraid of those who kill the body but cannot kill the soul. Instead, *fear the one who is able to destroy both **soul** and **body** in **hell**.*
>
> — Matthew 10:28

On the last day, God will judge everyone for their actions. Therefore, it is vital that we fear God as the judge he is because he has the power to send the sentenced souls to the final resting-place for sinners. For eternity!

Deal With Sin

In the gospel of Mark chapter 9, we are told what the consequences of sin are.

Wages of Sin - Mark 9:43-49

> 43 If your hand causes you to sin, cut it off! It is better for you to enter into life crippled than to have two hands and go into hell, to the unquenchable fire.
> 45 If your foot causes you to sin, cut it off! It is better to enter life lame than to have two feet and be thrown into hell.
> 47 If your eye causes you to sin, tear it out! It is better to enter into the kingdom of God with one eye than to have two eyes and be thrown into hell,

> 48 where their worm never dies and the fire
> is never quenched.
> 49 Everyone will be salted with fire.

It is better to deal with sin in your life rather than persevering in it. Get rid of everything that makes you stumble on the road.

Hell is the place where the holiness of God meets sin and sinners in its most refined form. Sin cannot be in the presence of God. In the same way as fire burns when the circumstances are the right; with oxygen, fuel and heat. Likewise, a consuming fire arises when sin and the holiness of God come into contact. Sin cannot last in the presence of God's holiness.

Hell Is Forever

Eternal Lost - Revelation 20:13-15

> 13 The sea gave up the dead that were in it, and Death and Hades gave up the dead that were in them, and each one was judged according to his deeds.

> [14] Then Death and Hades were thrown into
> the lake of fire. This is the second death–
> the lake of fire.
> [15] If anyone's name was not found written
> in the book of life, that person was thrown
> into the lake of fire.

The repository of damned souls is hell, and hell will be thrown into the burning lake of sulfur and brimstone at the final judgment. Do whatever you can to avoid ending up in this place.

Chapter 8

The Law and Sin

Does the Law apply today, haven't we been delivered from the Law?

The Law Applies Today!

> [17] Do not think that I have come to abolish the law or the prophets. *I have not come to abolish these things but to **fulfill them***.
>
> — Matthew 5:17

Just because we don't live during the Old Testament

time, does not mean that the Law has ceased or isn't of use anymore. The Law is timeless, the moral and righteousness reflected in it still applies. Jesus did not come to remove the Law but to fulfill it. The standard of morality and ethics today is the same as it was then, if not increased.

Justified by Keeping the Law?

> [20] For no one is declared righteous before him by the works of the law, for through the law comes the knowledge of sin.
>
> — Romans 3:20

Most people try to gain salvation by being *good enough*. They try to do the works that are good and try to avoid doing what is evil. The problem is that the more we try to do good and avoid doing evil, the more we realize we do not have the power to do so. We can not gain righteousness by keeping the Law, but instead get insight into how great sinners we are.

The Law Is a Measure

> [7] What shall we say then? Is the law sin? Absolutely not! Certainly, I would not have known sin except through the law. For indeed I would not have known what it means to desire something belonging to someone else if the law had not said, "Do not covet."
>
> — Romans 7:7

The Law is not evil in any way. It is you who live in sin and now has become aware of it. It's not the fault of the Law, but your ignorance. The Law is a measure by which we measure the distance between God's righteousness and our evil. Thereby the gap between God and us is revealed.

> [12] So then, the law is holy, and the commandment is holy, righteous, and good....[14] For we know that the law is spiritual– but I am unspiritual, sold into slavery to sin.
>
> — Romans 7:12, 14

So the Law is holy, right and good, yes even spiritual. By this, we discover that we are sold to slaves under sin, and discover our inability when we try to do good works.

Sin Is Crime Against the Law

> [4] Everyone who practices sin also practices lawlessness; indeed, sin is lawlessness.
>
> — 1 John 3:4

If the Law is the measure and represents what is righteous and just, then we must realize that breaking the Law is a sin. Sin can be translated as "missing the goal," we miss the goal of living a righteous and holy life.

> [12] For all who have sinned apart from the law will also perish apart from the law, and all who have sinned under the law will be judged by the law.
>
> — Romans 2:12

It doesn't matter whether you know the Law or not. Everyone has sinned, and everyone will either be judged or perish without righteousness.

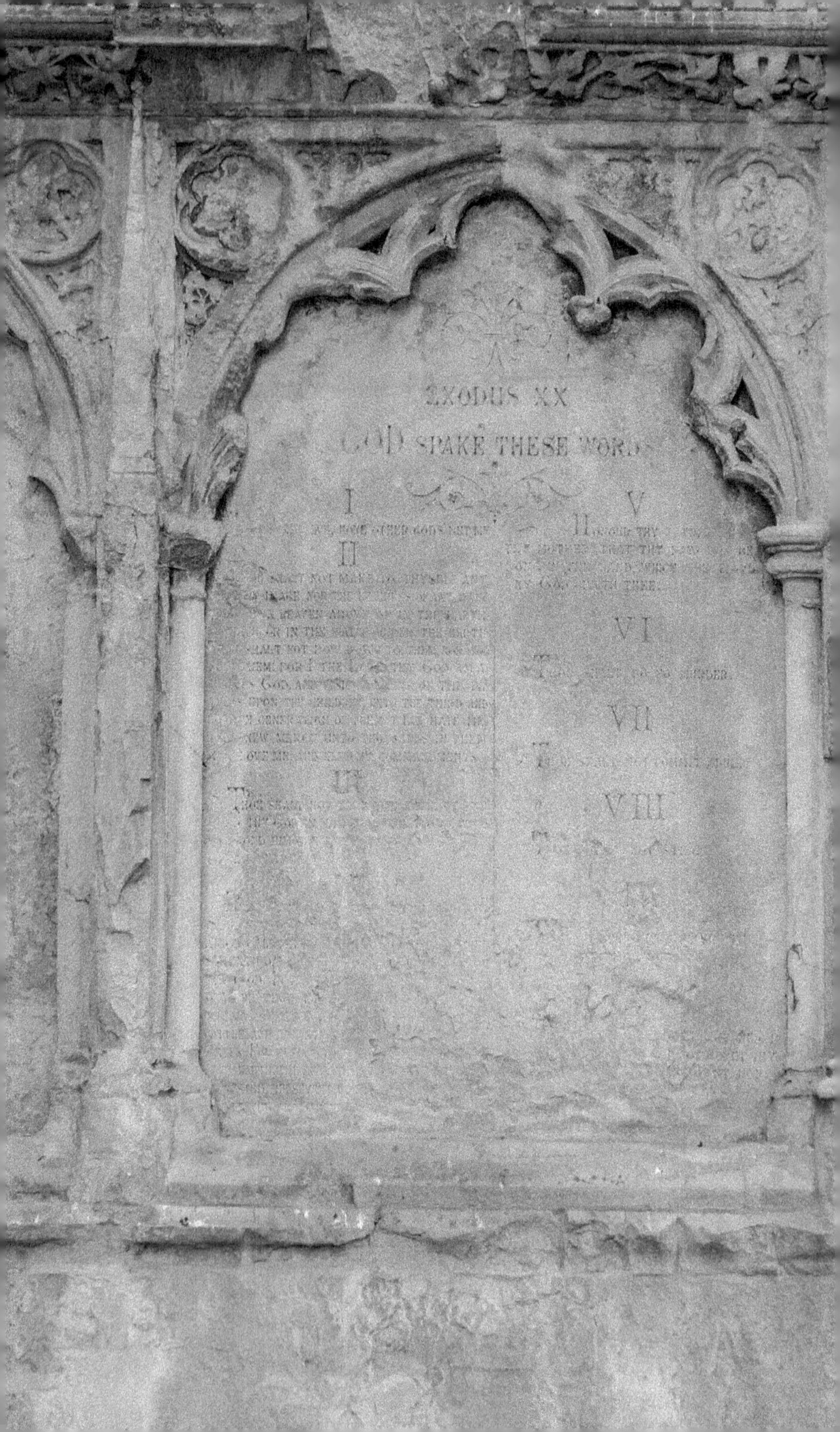
EXODUS XX
GOD SPAKE THESE WORDS
I
II
V
VI
VII
VIII

Chapter 9

First Commandment

The Old Testament

> [3] You shall have no other gods before me.
>
> — Exodus 20:3

The first of the Ten Commandments means that you should not have any other gods besides him. All gods that are not God are therefore idols. Everything that competes with God for your attention is idolatry. But exactly how is an idol defined and where are they hidden?

It's easy to imagine an idol as a statue or something that you can bow down before, but is that the correct definition of an idol? Below is a bible-text from Ezekiel 14 that defines idolatry.

Idolatry of the Heart – Ez 14:3-4

> 3 "Son of man, *these men have* ***erected*** *their* ***idols*** *in their* ***hearts*** *and placed the obstacle leading to their iniquity right before their faces*. Should I really allow them to seek me?
> 4 Therefore speak to them and say to them, 'This is what the sovereign LORD says: When any one from the house of Israel erects his idols in his **heart** and sets the obstacle leading to his iniquity before his face, and then consults a prophet, *I the LORD am determined to* ***answer*** *him personally* ***according*** *to the enormity of his* ***idolatry***.

An idol is not just a thing that you bow down in front of physically. An idol is something that you set up before you whatever it may be, not limited to physical things, but also intangible things: ideas, thought systems and more. An idol steps into the heart of a person and takes its dwelling there to lead that person astray into sin.

The New Testament

Can we find the first of the Ten Commandments in the New Testament?

> 10 Then Jesus said to him, "Go away, Satan! For it is written: 'You are to **worship** the Lord your God and **serve** only him.'"
>
> — Matthew 4:10

When Jesus was tempted by Satan in the desert, he used the scripture to resist the devil. From the above quotation we clearly see that it is only God whom you will a) worship and b) serve. Therefore, what we worship we will also serve. There is a connection between service and worship.

> 24 "No one can serve two masters, for either he will hate the one and love the

> other, or he will be devoted to the one and despise the other. You cannot serve God and money.
>
> — Matthew 6:24

You can only have one true master. There is more than one who claims the worship and service; therefore the idolatry takes place in the heart of us. These idols are competing with almighty God for attention.

> [13] No trial has overtaken you that is not faced by others. And God is faithful: He will not let you be tried beyond what you are able to bear, but with the trial will also provide a way out so that you may be able to endure it. [14] *So then, my dear friends, **flee** from **idolatry**.*
>
> — 1 Corinthians 10:13-14

Those that suffer from temptations in their lives have idols in their hearts. When someone is tempted, it is because of an idol that has lordship in their heart. When the idol rings the church bells to call for worship in your body, that's when you fall in sin.

Once the temptation wins, then the act of sin becomes

a worship service to that idol. Therefore, escape from all temptation because it has its roots in idolatry. Whatever idol that is set up before them, have been allowed to step into their hearts.

> [5] *So put to death whatever in your nature belongs to the earth:* sexual immorality, impurity, shameful passion, evil desire, and greed **which is idolatry**.
>
> — Colossians 3:5

We are commanded to kill all the desires that compete with almighty God for the first position in our hearts. All desires that we prioritize before following God is idolatry. Everything that we desire to satisfy us which is not God or of God are idols in our hearts.

A few examples from the quote above, sexual immorality. That is everything related to sex for our self-gratification; also all forms of sexual perversion are idols. Just as uncleanness, lust, and desire to commit evil. Even the love of money is idolatry.

Are You an Idolater?

Self-check: Are you a sinner, do you worship anything else except for God, which is to prioritize anything else above Him?

> [5] For you can be confident of this one thing: *that no person who is immoral, impure, or greedy (such a person* ***is an idolater****) has any inheritance in the kingdom of Christ and God.*
>
> — Ephesians 5:5

The Bible is clear that everyone who is an idolater will lose their eternity with God. Such have no inheritance in the kingdom of God. Idolaters must repent of their sins and renounce their idols, seek God to have their heart cleansed from all idols that have stepped inside their hearts.

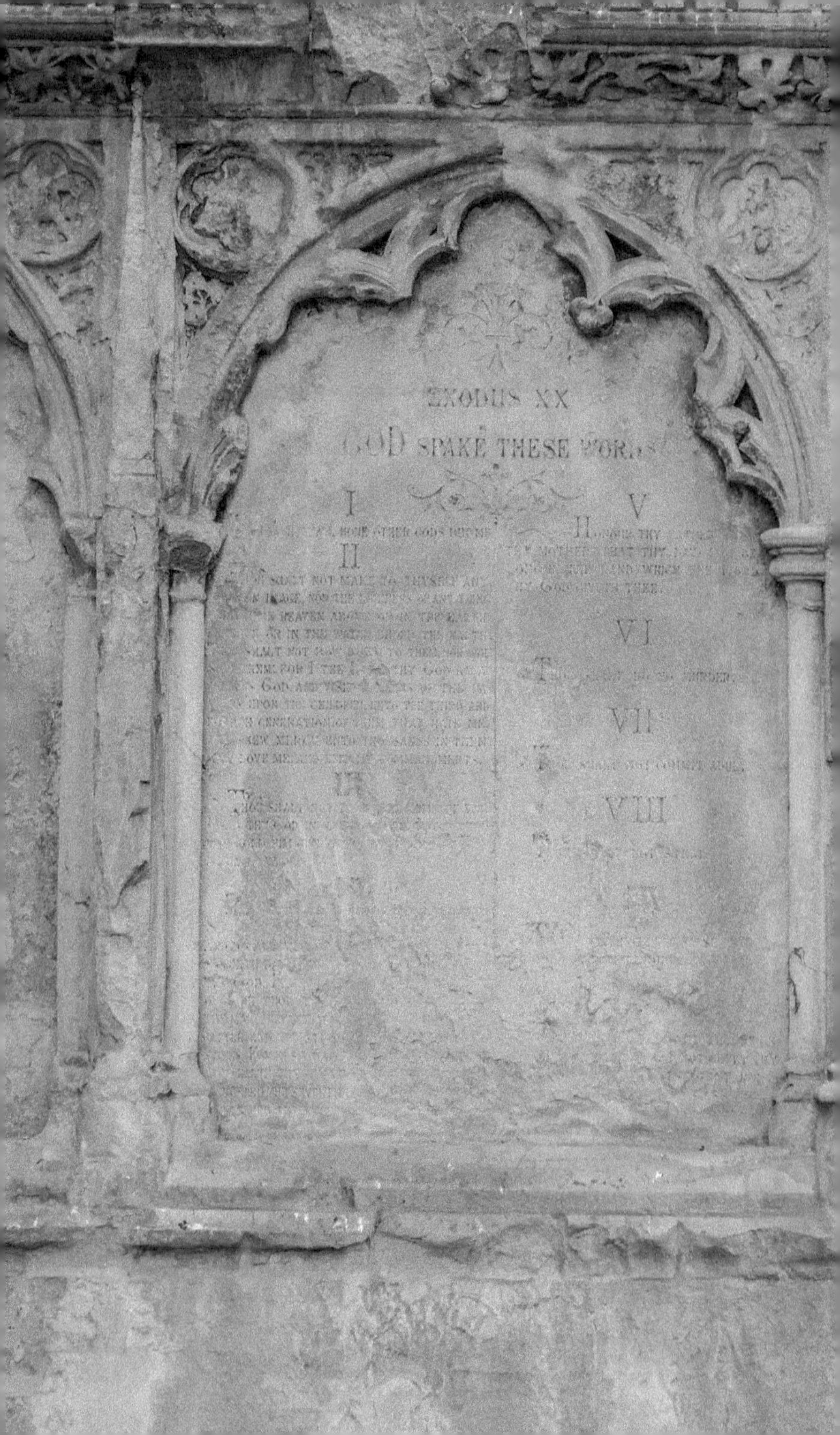
EXODUS XX
GOD SPAKE THESE WORDS
I
V
II
VI
VII
VIII

Chapter 10

Second Commandment

The Old Testament

4 "You shall not make for yourself a carved
image or any likeness of anything that is in
heaven above or that is on the earth
beneath or that is in the water below. 5 You
shall not bow down to them or serve them,
for I, the LORD, your God, am a jealous God,
responding to the transgression of fathers
by dealing with children to the third and
fourth generations of those who reject me,

> 6 and showing covenant faithfulness to a
> thousand generations of those who love
> me and keep my commandments.
>
> — Exodus 20:4-6

During the time of the Old Testament, nobody was allowed to set up idols such as statues or similar to worship.

The New Testament

Another way to carve out idols for oneself is to make a customized gospel according to your liking or to create "another Jesus," that suits your taste and cravings. The Bible commands us to receive the Gospel and Jesus the way he is.

> 3 For there will be a time when people will
> not tolerate sound teaching. *Instead,*
> ***following their own desires****, they will*
> *accumulate teachers for themselves,*
> *because they have an insatiable curiosity*
> *to hear new things.*
> 4 *And they will* ***turn***

> ***away*** *from hearing* **the truth**, but on the other hand they will turn aside to myths.
>
> — 2 Timothy 4:3-4

People with idols in their hearts tend to dislike the truth. They gather teachers and ministers who preach only their favorite passages from the Bible. Those things they like themselves and that is consistent with the idols of their hearts.

> [3] But I am afraid that just as the serpent deceived Eve by his treachery, your minds may be led astray from a sincere and pure devotion to Christ. [4] For if someone comes and proclaims **another Jesus** different from the one we proclaimed, or if you receive a **different spirit** than the one you received, or a **different gospel** than the one you accepted, *you put up with it well enough!*
>
> — 2 Corinthians 11:3-4

It's easy to be led astray from the true faith and the true Gospel, to satisfy the selfish hidden lusts of the heart. Therefore, heresies and false teachers arise that leads the multitudes astray. When you choose only the pieces that you like in the Bible and selectively listen to the parts of Jesus' teachings that suit your agenda, you are being led away from God.

> [8] But even if we (or an angel from heaven) should preach **a gospel contrary** to the one we preached to you, let him be condemned to hell! [9] As we have said before, and now I say again, *if any one is preaching to you a **gospel contrary** to what you received, **let him be condemned** to **hell**!*
>
> — Galatians 1:8-9

Anyone preaching another gospel, and carving out a false image of Jesus other than the one contained in the scripture of God is accursed.

Have You Made a False Image?

> [22] Who is the liar but the person who denies that Jesus is the Christ? *This one is **the antichrist**: the person who denies the Father and the Son.*
>
> — 1 John 2:22

Have you made yourself a false image of Jesus? I am

not saying you can not have a painting, porcelain figure or any other object of art, that is a piece of work that depicts Jesus. However, if you have created your own interpretation of who Jesus is, compared to the biblical Jesus, and made up your own way of salvation. Then you deny God, the Father, and the Son. You need to repent of your heresy, confess it as a sin and come back to obedience to the Word of God.

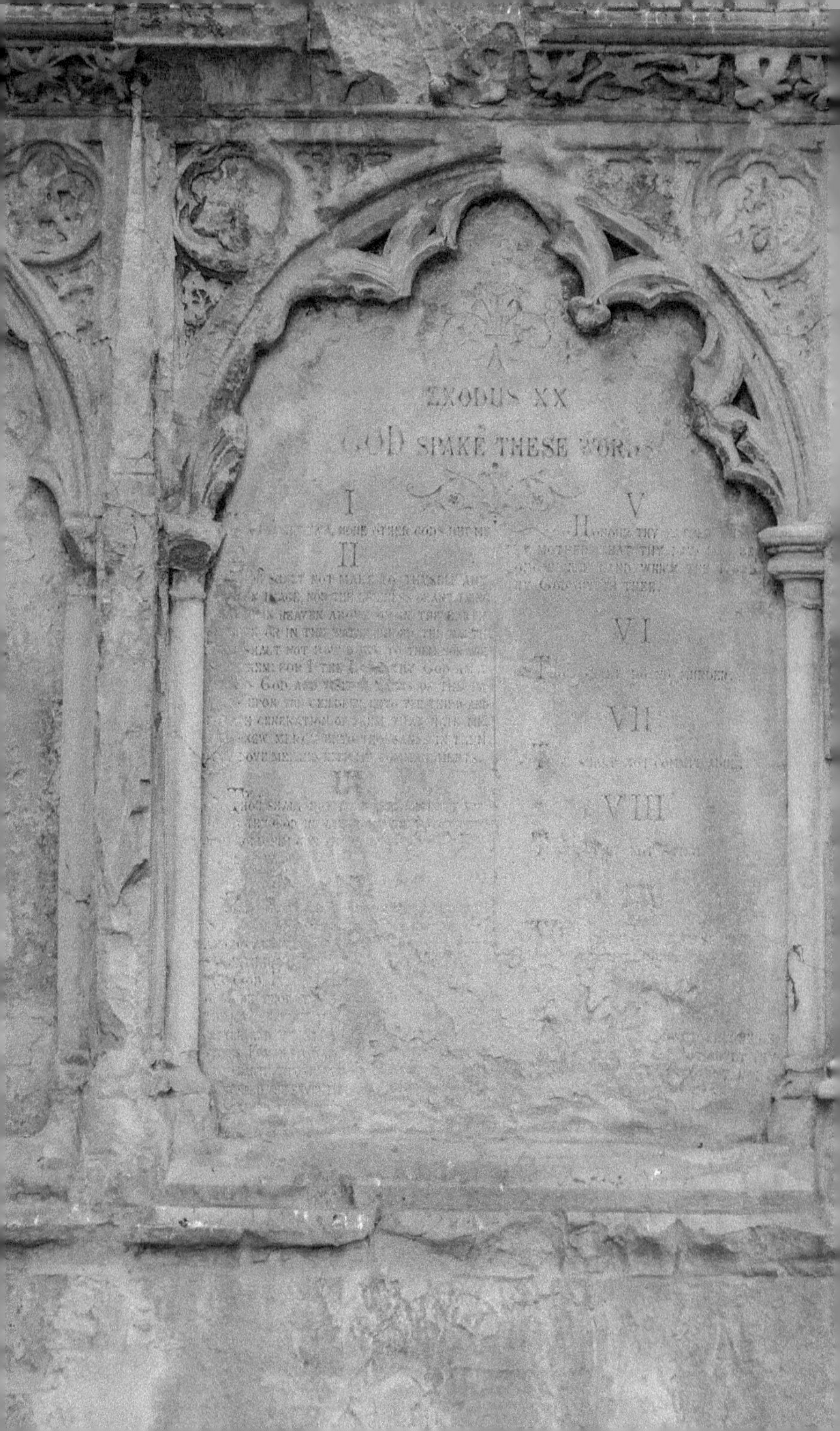
EXODUS XX
GOD SPAKE THESE WORDS
I
II
V
VI
VII
VIII

Chapter 11

Third Commandment

The Old Testament

> [7] You shall not take the name of the LORD your God in vain, for the LORD will not hold guiltless anyone who takes his name in vain.
>
> — Exodus 20:7

Most people think that we are not supposed to curse God with verbal blasphemies. But the third commandment is way stronger than that; we shall not take God's name in vain. What does it mean to take the name of God in vain?

One way to take the name of God in vain is to use it as an expletive, instead of using profane cussing. Another way is, to talk about God, in a way that is degrading him, or just without any respect for who he is. That is a vain use of the name of God.

The New Testament

In the New Testament, the understanding of misusing the name of God is much broader.

> [34] *But I say to you, do not take **oaths** at all–* not by heaven, because it is the throne of God, [35] not by earth, because it is his footstool, and not by Jerusalem, because it is the city of the great King.
>
> — Matthew 5:34-35

As in the Old Testament, we should not mindlessly use the name of God. Moreover, we are not supposed to take the name of God in vain by swearing by it, neither are we supposed to take oaths. Best is if we don't take vows at all if we for some reason would break them.

We are also taught not to swear by the heavens or the earth either. The name of God should always be used with respect, not in a careless way or as a nonsense word.

How Do We Live?

> [1] Those who are under the yoke as slaves must regard their own masters as deserving of full respect. *This will prevent the name of God and Christian teaching from being* ***discredited***.
>
> — 1 Timothy 6:1

As representatives of God on earth, we need to realize that our lifestyle is a witness. It is important to note that calling our selves the children of God, and then misbehave, will discredit God. We should live in such a way that the name of God has a good reputation. If we have someone in authority over us in this world, such as the boss at work, our actions bear witness of who we are. Therefore we should be reliable, trustworthy and good ambassadors to the kingdom of God.

Have You Discredited God?

Then you need to confess your sin and ask God for his forgiveness. Then you will watch your tongue, think about how you behave and always keep the name of God in mind.

EXODUS XX
SPAKE THESE
I
V
II
VI
VII
VIII

Chapter 12

Fourth Commandment

The Old Testament

> 8 "Remember the Sabbath day to set it
> apart as holy. 9 For six days you may labor
> and do all your work, 10 but the seventh
> day is a Sabbath to the LORD your God; on
> it you shall not do any work, you, or your
> son, or your daughter, or your male
> servant, or your female servant, or your
> cattle, or the resident foreigner who is in
> your gates. 11 For in six days the LORD

> made the heavens and the earth and the sea and all that is in them, and he rested on the seventh day; therefore the LORD blessed the Sabbath day and set it apart as holy.
>
> — Exodus 20:8-11

In the Old Testament, God created the seventh day so that you could rest and sanctify that day for God.

The New Testament

In the New Testament, the Sabbath has a new and much more profound meaning. If we were to keep the Sabbath commandment literally, then we must understand that Sunday is the wrong day for the Sabbath. Sunday is a church tradition from the 2nd century. Then it's easy to conclude that the holy day has to be Saturday, the day when the Jews celebrate Sabbath. The problem here is that Saturday is also the wrong day. If we need to go to the bottom, we have to understand that the Gregorian calendar is wrong. The mosaic calendar of the Old Testament is not sun-based, but moon-based. This fundamentally changes how we need to calculate the dates; it would be necessary to study the Law of Moses very well to comply. This kind of interpretation of the Bible would be legalistic.

Jesus Is the Lord of the Sabbath

> 27 Then he said to them, "*The Sabbath was*
> *made for people, not people for the*
> *Sabbath.* 28 *For this reason the Son of Man*
> *(Jesus) is* ***lord even of the Sabbath***."
>
> — Mark 2:27-28

Jesus clearly says that he is the Lord of the Sabbath and that the Sabbath was made for man, and not the other way around. That implies that God has created a resting place for us to enter into.

> 9 Consequently a Sabbath rest remains for
> the people of God. 10 For the one who
> enters God's rest has also rested from his
> works, just as God did from his own works.
> 11 Thus we must make every effort to enter
> that rest, so that no one may fall by

> following the same pattern of
> disobedience.
>
> — Hebrews 4:9-11

The real Sabbath rest is to get to know Jesus Christ. Not just proclaiming him but fully believing and trusting in him. That he is the one, who carries us. We must understand that it is not a day in the week, but a place in God, to enter into this resting-place.

That place is with Jesus in his kingdom, where we can rest ourselves from our works, where it is the grace of God that carries us. Not seeking to find this resting-place is disobedience to God, because otherwise, we try to hold on to our works.

Have You Entered Into the Sabbath?

Have you found the Sabbath? To find the resting-place of the Sabbath, we must believe in Jesus as well as obey God to be let in. If you have not found that rest yet, you need to start to obey God and seek the Sabbath. Eventually, you may also need to repent and receive Jesus as Lord and get to know him.

EXODUS XX
GOD SPAKE THESE WORDS
I
V
II
VI
THOU SHALT DO NO MURDER.
VII
VIII

Chapter 13

Fifth Commandment

The Old Testament

> 12 "Honor your father and your mother, that you may live a long time in the land the LORD your God is giving to you.
>
> — Exodus 20:12

The Old Testament says that we should honor our parents. It could mean that you would not be disobedient to them. But also be kind to them and take care of them when they get old. It's blessed by God to honor your parents.

The New Testament

> [20] *Children, obey your parents in everything, for this is **pleasing** in the Lord.*
>
> — Colossians 3:20

Even in the New Testament, we find verses in the Bible that say the same thing, that it is the will of God that children should submit to their parents and honor them.

Family Relationships – Ephesians 6:1-4

> [1] Children, obey your parents in the Lord for this is right.
> [2] "Honor your father and mother," which is the first commandment accompanied by a promise, namely,
> [3] "that it may go well with you and that you will live a long time on the earth."
> [4] Fathers, do not provoke your children to anger, but raise them up in the discipline and instruction of the Lord.

Since God created us to live and to have a family, it is the will of God that we should have good relationships with one another. This is reflected in that the children are supposed to submit to their parents, and later in life when they can not take care of themselves, support them.

According to Ephesians 6:1, it is evident that it is in the Lord that the children should submit to their parents. Thus, obey the parents always, except if it is evident that what they demand is wrong.

Parents are also encouraged to raise and foster the children in the instruction of the Lord so that they can grow up and become secure and confident individuals. It's essential that parents do not mistreat their children or provoke them but love them.

Do You Honor Your Parents?

If you are living in such a way that you do not care about your parents or insult them, then you live in sin and need to repent. In the sense that the parents have hurt you, you need to forgive them in Jesus name.

EXODUS XX
SPAKE THESE WOR
I
V
II
VI
VII
VIII

Chapter 14

Sixth Commandment

The Old Testament

> [13] You shall not murder.
>
> — Exodus 20:13

The sixth commandment is self-explanatory, you should not murder. In the Old Testament, the death penalty was applied, but killing in a war did not count as murder. That implies there was a difference between killing and murdering; when innocent people were killed it counted as murder.

The New Testament

In the New Testament, the commandment has been sharpened significantly. It's not just about killing people physically but also mentally and emotionally.

> [15] Whosoever hates his brother is a murderer: and you know that no murderer has eternal life abiding in him.
>
> — 1 John 3:15 (KJV)

Everything we do is motivated by our hearts. We say nothing and do nothing without having our hearts at it. The motive behind all murder is hatred. Hate is the root of murder.

Therefore, the one who hates his neighbor is a murderer, and the person who lives in hatred can not inherit eternal life. Hate and eternal life are not compatible.

Hate Is Murder - Matthew 5:21-22

> [21] You have heard that it was said to an older generation, "Do not murder," and whoever

> murders will be subjected to judgment.
> [22] But I say to you that anyone who is angry with a brother will be subjected to judgment. And whoever insults a brother will be brought before the council, and whoever says "Fool" will be sent to fiery hell.

To live in anger towards other people and to hold on to unforgiveness is murder in the eyes of God.

Are You a Murderer?

If you live in anger, hate or hold on to unforgiveness, then you have sinned. The Bible is clear, the one who does so is a murderer, and no murderer can have eternal life.

If you have committed this sin, then you must repent of your sin and ask God for forgiveness. Forgive whoever you have not forgiven, and receive Jesus as Lord.

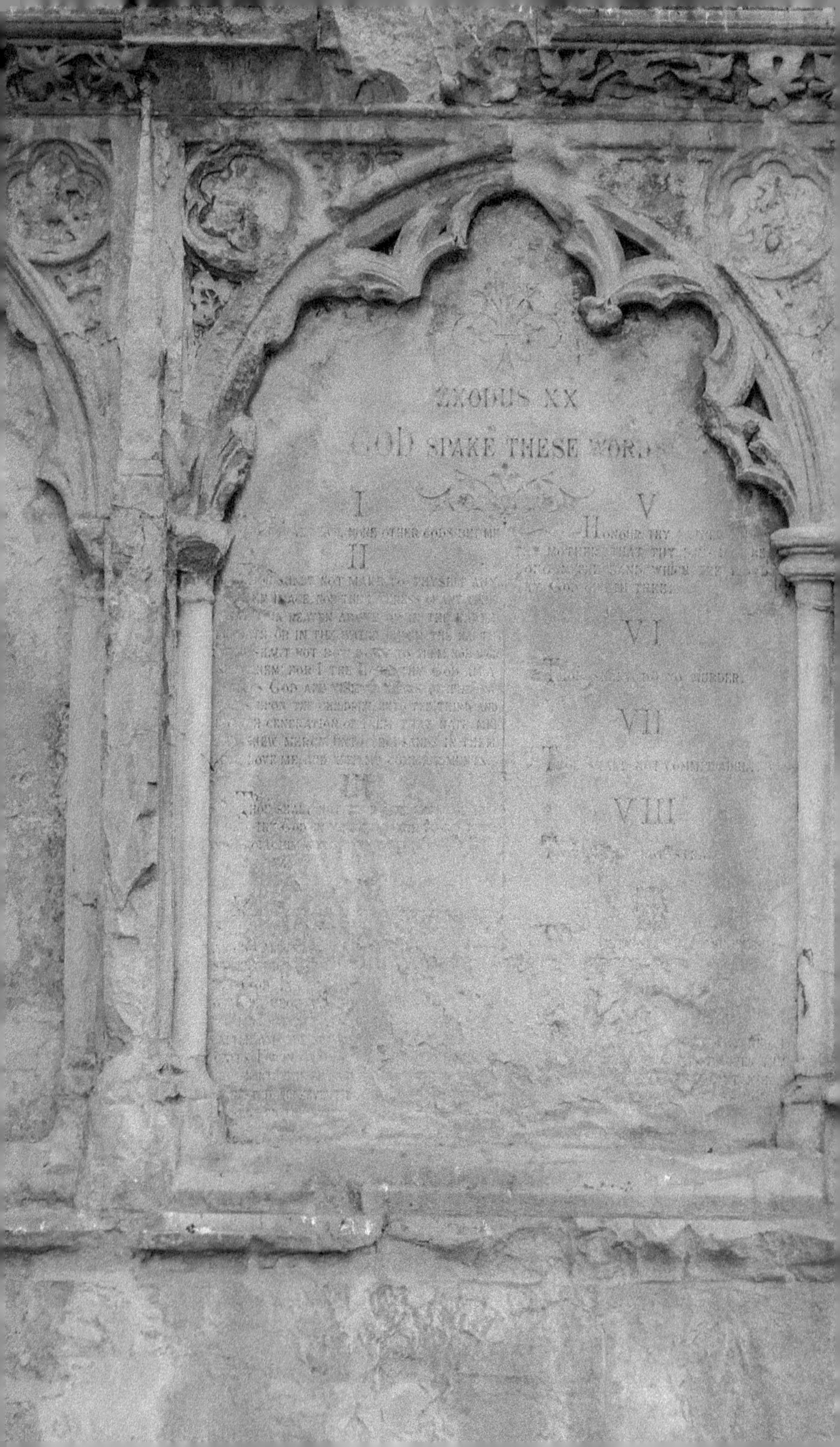
EXODUS XX
GOD SPAKE THESE
I
V
II
VI
VII
VIII

Chapter 15

Seventh Commandment

The Old Testament

> [14] You shall not commit adultery.
>
> — Exodus 20:14

According to Mosaic law, when someone within a marriage fornicated with a person outside of the covenant, it was a breach of the marriage, and it was called adultery. Adultery means to break the marriage union and is a severe sin.

The New Testament

In the New Testament, the understanding of adultery is sharpened once again.

Adultery at Heart - Matthew 5:27-28

> 27 You have heard that it was said, "Do not commit adultery."
> 28 But I say to you that whoever looks at a woman to desire her has already committed adultery with her in his heart.

The Bible says that all our actions begin with intentions in our hearts. It starts with thoughts that are then expressed in actions. Looking at a married woman with sexual desires is adultery since it has already taken place in the mind. Similarly, it is fornication to see at an unmarried woman with sexual desires when it begins at heart.

This commandment also goes in reverse. If a woman looks at a man with sexual desires, it is also adultery or fornication at heart and counts as a sin.

Divorce - Matthew 5:31-32

> 31 It was said, "Whoever divorces his wife must give her a legal document."
> 32 But I say to you that everyone who divorces his wife, except for immorality, makes her commit adultery, and whoever marries a divorced woman commits adultery.

We also get an updated view on divorce. In the Old Testament, they could divorce and remarry. Jesus says in the New Testament that someone who separates for any reason other than sexual sin is guilty of adultery.

Are You an Adulterer?

Are you a fornicator or adulterer? All sin begins in the heart! Have you had sexual desires at heart about another person that is not your spouse? In that case, you are a fornicator or an adulterer. You need to repent of your sin and ask God for forgiveness and receive Jesus as Savior and Lord.

EXODUS XX
GOD SPAKE THESE
I
II
V
VI
VII
VIII

Chapter 16

Eighth Commandment

The Old Testament

> 15 You shall not steal.
>
> — Exodus 20:15

The eighth commandment is easy! You should not steal, that is to take what belongs to others.

The New Testament

> 19 You know the commandments: "Do not

> murder, do not commit adultery, **do not steal**, do not give false testimony, **do not defraud**, honor your father and mother."
>
> — Mark 10:19

In the New Testament, we can read that the same commandment is repeated: You should not steal. But it is also sharpened: You should not take away anything that belongs to someone else, it's not just about theft but also about lesser things.

> 28 The one who steals must steal no longer; rather he must labor, doing good with his own hands, so that he may have something to share with the one who has need.
>
> — Ephesians 4:28

The thief is commanded to change the direction of his life. Instead of taking from others what was earned the hard way, they are supposed to start working for their livelihood and start to do good. Notice that there is no room for Robin Hood mentality! The thief should stop stealing and be generous with their hard-earned nickels!

Are You a Thief?

> 10 **thieves**, the **greedy**, drunkards, the verbally abusive, and **swindlers** will not inherit the kingdom of God.
>
> — 1 Corinthians 6:10

Have you ever stolen anything? Even something small, maybe shoplifted just a candy bar? Then you're a thief. Perhaps you might be a corrupt politician who is generous with others money, but not with your own?

Or maybe you want to live on the welfare of others but do not contribute. Note that there is a difference in not wishing to contribute and not being able to.

But if you are a thief, greedy or an exploiter, you must repent before God and ask for the forgiveness of sins. Then you can be saved and forgiven through Jesus Christ.

EXODUS XX
GOD SPAKE THESE
I
V
II
VI
VII
VIII

Chapter 17

Ninth Commandment

The Old Testament

> [16] You shall not give false testimony
> against your neighbor.
>
> — Exodus 20:16

Under the Mosaic law, it was severe to talk trash about others and to gossip. Everything that was said about someone counted as a legally binding testimony.

The New Testament

In the New Testament, it is equally important to control your tongue, not to be tempted to gossip or to let slander come out your mouth uncontrolled.

> [8] But now, put off all such things as anger, rage, malice, **slander**, **abusive language from your mouth**.
>
> — Colossians 3:8

The Untidy Tongue - James 3:5-10 (KJV)

You are not supposed to be divided in your heart, nor in your speech. Everything you say counts, and you will be judged for that. Therefore everything you say should be in unison.

> [5] Even so the tongue is a little member, and boasts great things. Behold, how great a matter a little fire kindles!
> [6] And the tongue is a fire, a world of iniquity: so is the tongue among our members, that it defiles the whole body, and sets on fire the course of nature; and it is set on fire of

> hell.
> [7] For every kind of beasts, and of birds,
> and of serpents, and of things in the sea,
> is tamed, and has been tamed of mankind:
> [8] But the tongue can no man tame; it is an
> unruly evil, full of deadly poison.
> [9] Therewith bless we God, even the Father;
> and therewith curse we men, which are
> made after the similitude of God.
> [10] Out of the same mouth proceeds blessing
> and cursing. My brothers, these things ought
> not so to be.

Try to understand this: Don't be defiled. What defiles you may not be what you eat, not always what you do, but what you say. Please keep your mouth-slurry in check!

> [11] What defiles a person is not what goes into the mouth; it is what comes out of the mouth that defiles a person.
>
> — Matthew 15:11

Everything unclean you say with your mouth makes your heart and persona filthy. Whether it's slander, gossip, trash- or dirty talk, or whatever it may be.

Are You a Babbler?

If you're a slanderer, trash-talker or just a common chatter-nagger, you'll need to repent to Jesus for salvation, deliverance, and forgiveness.

EXODUS XX
GOD SPAKE THESE WOR
I
V
II
VI
VII
VIII

Chapter 18

Tenth Commandment

The Old Testament

> [17] "You shall not covet your neighbor's house. You shall not covet your neighbor's wife, nor his male servant, nor his female servant, nor his ox, nor his donkey, nor anything that belongs to your neighbor."
>
> — Exodus 20:17

The last of the Ten Commandments is: You should not covet. In this commandment, we see a list of things you should not covet, but it ends with "...nor anything that belongs to your neighbor." That is, you should not go around and have cravings for anyone else's belongings. Do not be dissatisfied and jealous, be happy and satisfied with what you have.

The New Testament

In the New Testament, we see the importance of not having desires because they lead us astray. We get lead away from God and into idolatry. If we follow our worldly lusts, we will get lost.

Covetousness Leads to Fall - 1 Corinthians 10:3-6

> 3 and all ate the same spiritual food,
> 4 and all drank the same spiritual drink. For they were all drinking from the spiritual rock that followed them, and the rock was Christ.
> 5 But God was not pleased with most of them, for they were cut down in the wilderness.
> 6 These things happened as examples for us, *so that we will* ***not crave*** *evil things as they did.*

The Israelites who wandered in the desert from Egypt never entered the promised land, at least not the first generation. The reason was that they only followed their cravings, instead of following God and having their eyes set on Him. That way, they have become an example for us today, not to let our desires rule us.

> 2:3 among whom all of us also formerly lived out our lives in the cravings of our flesh, indulging the desires of the flesh and the mind, and were by nature children of wrath even as the rest...4:22 You were taught with reference to your former way of life to lay aside the old man who is being corrupted in accordance with deceitful desires,
>
> — Ephesians 2:3, 4:22

All people have once been the children of wrath, who followed their flesh and whatever it would lust after.

It's part of our fallen nature, to only do what gives us quick and short-term satisfaction but often with long-term negative consequences.

Therefore, God has called us to lay off our desires, as it deceives us and leads us to destruction in the long run.

> [18] Others are the ones sown among thorns: They are those who hear the word, [19] but worldly cares, the seductiveness of wealth, and the desire for other things come in and choke the word, and it produces nothing.
>
> — Mark 4:18-19

It is essential to review what soil quality we are. If we hear the word of God but let worldly matters take over, then the word becomes unfruitful. The result of this is that the desires rule us and leads us astray.

> [16] because all that is in the world (the desire of the flesh and the desire of the eyes and the arrogance produced by material possessions) is not from the Father, but is from the world. [17] *And the world is passing away with all its desires, but the person who does the will of God* ***remains forever***.
>
> — 1 John 2:16-17

Whatever is not of God is of the world. If we follow what is of the world, then we do not obey God but our desires.

To follow what the flesh wants, fornication and forbidden pleasure, what the eyes wish for, whatever it may be. As well as the pride over what we gained in life, so that we may think of ourselves as better than others. All of this has an end to it, and if we follow the desires, we will end the same way. What we should do instead is the will of God!

> 22 But keep away from youthful passions,
> and pursue righteousness, faithfulness,
> love, and peace, in company with others
> who call on the Lord from a pure heart.
>
> — 2 Timothy 2:22

Flee away from all temptations and what else that leads you astray. Disregard the short-term pleasures for the benefit of fellowship with those who love the Lord, and learn to love them through God.

Seek to have a pure heart. Then we can love our fellow neighbors instead of selfishly satisfying our desires, which spreads pain and suffering around the world.

> [24] Now those who belong to Christ have crucified the flesh with its passions and desires.
>
> — Galatians 5:24

Are You Into Covetousness?

Is it the short-term pleasure and the satisfaction that tempts you? Then you live for yourself and not for your neighbor, by doing so, you sin against both God and man.

You need to repent of your sin and make Jesus Lord and Savior in your life. When you receive him, he becomes your source of satisfaction. Jesus is the water of life and the brook that never dries out.

Chapter 19

Salvation

What Does Salvation Mean?

Lets read a text from Isaiah chapter 53; it's a prophetic contemplative text about what Jesus has done for us.

Salvation – Isaiah 53:10-11 (KJV)

> 10 Yet it pleased the Lord to bruise him; he
> has put him to grief: *when you shall make*
> *his soul an* ***offering for sin***, he shall see

> his seed, he shall prolong his days, and the pleasure of the Lord shall prosper in his hand.
> [11] He shall see of the travail of his soul, and shall be satisfied: *by his knowledge shall my righteous servant* ***justify*** *many; for he shall bear their* ***iniquities***.

The root word to "salvation" is "save." According to Mariam-websters dictionary "save" means, among other things:

- to rescue or deliver from danger or harm
- to preserve or guard against injury, destruction, or loss
- to avoid unnecessary waste

This comes from the consequences of sin. A sinner will according to the Bible be judged and punished with eternal flames of fire. Thereby salvation results in: being preserved, delivered or avoid having their soul being wasted.

The meaning of "being saved" in the Bible is vast. Salvation includes being redeemed from sin, but also to be healed, restored and liberated in all areas. Salvation is total.

The Salvation of God Revealed

> [11] For the grace of God has appeared,
> bringing salvation to all people.
>
> — Titus 2:11

God has revealed the way of salvation through Jesus Christ by his grace. The salvation that can set all people free from the devil's oppression and the slavery to sin.

It is by the grace of God that salvation is available. In no way by ourselves or our accomplishment. Only through the mercy of God.

Jesus Is the Source of Salvation

> [9] And by being perfected in this way, he
> (Jesus) became the source of eternal
> salvation to all who obey him,
>
> — Hebrews 5:9

That Jesus was perfected, points to the work performed on the Cross of Calvary when Jesus was crucified, died and resurrected from the dead. It is Jesus who is the sacrifice for all the sin in the world.

As it was stated in the contemplative text, "*when you shall make his soul an offering for sin, he shall see his seed.*" It is Jesus who is the sacrifice, and it is by his work that we can be saved.

The Good News

> [16] For I am not ashamed of the gospel, *for it is God's* ***power*** *for* ***salvation*** *to everyone who believes*, to the Jew first and also to the Greek.
>
> — Romans 1:16

The Gospel is "The Good News." The message that everyone can be saved by grace, for those who believe in Jesus and obey his will. The Gospel and everything related to that is the teaching of salvation as the power of God.

Grace and salvation have no limits, it applies to Jews

as well as anyone else, regardless of sex, nationality or ethnicity.

Chapter 20

Transition to Light

Delivered From Darkness Into Light

We begin this chapter with another contemplative text from the prophet Isaiah, chapter 9. Jesus as the bright light.

The Bright Light – Isaiah 9:2-4

> [2] *The people walking in darkness see a*
> ***bright light**; **light shines** on those who*
> *live in a land of deep darkness.* [3] You

> have enlarged the nation; you give them great joy. They rejoice in your presence as harvesters rejoice; as warriors celebrate when they divide up the plunder.
> [4] *For their* ***oppressive yoke*** *and the* ***club that strikes their shoulders, the cudgel*** *the oppressor uses on them,* ***you have shattered****, as in the day of Midian's defeat.*

Salvation is a journey from a walk in darkness during slavery, yoke, and hostage, to be unshackled from the oppression of darkness and thereby entering into light. Jesus is the great light that rose like the sun for humanity when God sent him to earth.

Jesus Sent as Savior

> [17] For God did not send his Son into the world to condemn the world, but that the world should be saved through him.
>
> — John 3:17

The purpose of sending Jesus was not to judge those who were in slavery by the oppressors. On the contrary, he came to save the world, for those who receive him, those who make Jesus the sacrifice for their sins.

> 9 For God did not destine us for wrath but
> for gaining salvation through our Lord
> Jesus Christ.
>
> — 1 Thessalonians 5:9

God has decided about those who received Jesus as savior, that they should not suffer from the wrath of judgment. They should escape the judgment of the sinners, and instead win the salvation that is available through Jesus.

Transferred to the Kingdom of God

> 13 He delivered us from the power of
> darkness and transferred us to the
> kingdom of the Son he loves, 14 in whom we
> have redemption, the forgiveness of sins.
>
> — Colossians 1:13-14

Before you received salvation, you walked in the darkness; you were in the valley of death. In that darkness, you were a slave under sin, tortured by

Satan.

When you received Jesus as savior, he freed you from slavery and broke the power of Satan over your life. You received forgiveness of sins, and the yoke was removed from your shoulders.

When this happened, God put you as a free person in the Kingdom of Jesus. That is how you have gone from darkness to light. Jesus is that light, through which the work of salvation was carried out on the Cross of Calvary.

Chapter 21

Receive Salvation

How Do I Get Saved?

Lets read a text from Isaiah chapter 53. It is a prophetic, contemplative text about what Jesus took for us on the Cross.

Jesus in Our Place – Isaiah 53:5-7

> 5 He was wounded because of our rebellious deeds, crushed because of our sins; he endured punishment that made us well;

> because of his wounds we have been healed.
> [6] All of us had wandered off like sheep; each of us had strayed off on his own path, but the LORD caused the sin of all of us to attack him.
> [7] He was treated harshly and afflicted, but he did not even open his mouth. Like a lamb led to the slaughtering block, like a sheep silent before her shearers, he did not even open his mouth.

Salvation is not something that comes by itself. It is something we receive from God as a gift. Receiving salvation is the beginning of something new in your life.

If now the punishment and the debts are imposed on Jesus for our sins, how do I have this applied in my own life to get saved?

Believe in Jesus

> [30] Then he brought them outside and asked, "Sirs, what must I do to be saved?" [31] They

> replied, "***Believe*** *in the Lord Jesus and you will be* ***saved****, you and your household.*"
>
> — Acts 16:30-31

The foundation for salvation is to believe in Jesus. It is through the faith in him that we gain access to the grace of God.

Believing God about something does not mean that we only *believe* intellectually or emotionally in the existence of God. The faith is very specific; it is about a relationship.

To believe in God, is to have trust in God, that he responds to us as we reach out to him.

Confess Jesus as Lord

> 9 because *if you confess with your mouth that Jesus is Lord and believe in your heart that God raised him from the dead, you will be* ***saved***.
>
> — Romans 10:9

Confession is of the utmost importance. If you choose to believe that Jesus is your savior, it should also be confessed with your mouth. What your mouth speaks is what you have in your heart.

We believe Jesus died on the Cross for our sins as the sacrificial lamb of God. We also believe that God raised Jesus from the dead, and thereby won an eternal victory over death and evil.

Let Yourself be Baptized

> [16] *The one who believes and is baptized will be* ***saved***, but the one who does not believe will be condemned.
>
> — Mark 16:16

Baptism belongs together with faith and salvation. Baptism is a symbol of burial, which means that we who receive salvation have been crucified, dead, buried, and raised with Christ from our sins.

If we receive salvation from God and believe him, we will be saved by dying from our evil desires through the blood that was shed on the Cross of Calvary.

You must understand that baptism without faith is worthless, a formal outwardly ritual does not save anyone from anything.

Chapter 22

Fulfill Salvation

Finish Your Course!

In second Timothy 4, Paul explains that we need to fulfill our salvation by running the race.

Run the Race – 2 Timothy 4:6-8

> [6] For I am already being poured out as an offering, and the time for me to depart is at hand.
> [7]*I have* ***competed well****; I have* ***finished the***

> ***race***; *I have* ***kept the faith***!
> [8] Finally the crown of righteousness is reserved for me. The Lord, the righteous Judge, will award it to me in that day– and not to me only, but also to all who have set their affection on his appearing.

We who have received the salvation must be aware that we are on a journey. This trip consists of:

1. fight the good fight
2. complete the race
3. preserve your faith

Once Saved, Always Saved?

> [13] *But the person who* ***endures*** *to the end will be* ***saved***.
>
> — Matthew 24:13

Once saved always saved!? Is this statement correct? Just because you received salvation once, does that mean that you always will remain saved?

The greatest lie within the church, and especially within

the evangelical church community, is that you remain saved just because you once prayed the salvation prayer.

The Bible clearly states; that the one that endures to the end will be saved, not the one who gives up or who stops walking the narrow path.

The Good Will of God

> [12] So then, my dear friends, just as you have always obeyed, not only in my presence but even more in my absence, *continue working out your* ***salvation*** *with awe and reverence,* [13] *for the one bringing forth in you both the* ***desire and the effort****– for the sake of* ***his good pleasure****– is God.*
>
> — Philippians 2:12-13

It is the good will of God that we should be saved! It is God who through his grace works salvation in us. But this working within us does not affect unless we are obedient to God.

God is the one who judges us; we must obey and fear God. We are commanded to work on our salvation, not so that we have an opportunity to earn salvation. But it is up to us, to cooperate with God so that his good will can happen.

Sanctification Through the Truth

> [13] But we are bound to give thanks always to God for you, brothers beloved of the Lord, because *God has from the beginning chosen you to **salvation** through sanctification of **the Spirit** and **belief of the truth**:*
>
> — 2 Thessalonians 2:13 (KJV)

God has determined that we should be saved. For this to happen, we need to believe the truth. When we believe the truth, we will be sanctified by the Spirit.

There is a connection between completing salvation and being sanctified by the Spirit, through the truth. As we learn and understand the truth, the Holy Spirit can work salvation in us through the process of sanctification.

Preserved Unto Salvation

> [5] who by God's power are **protected through faith** for a **salvation** ready to be revealed in the last time.
>
> — 1 Peter 1:5

God will through faith preserve us with his power to fulfill salvation. He is the only one that is mighty to do that.

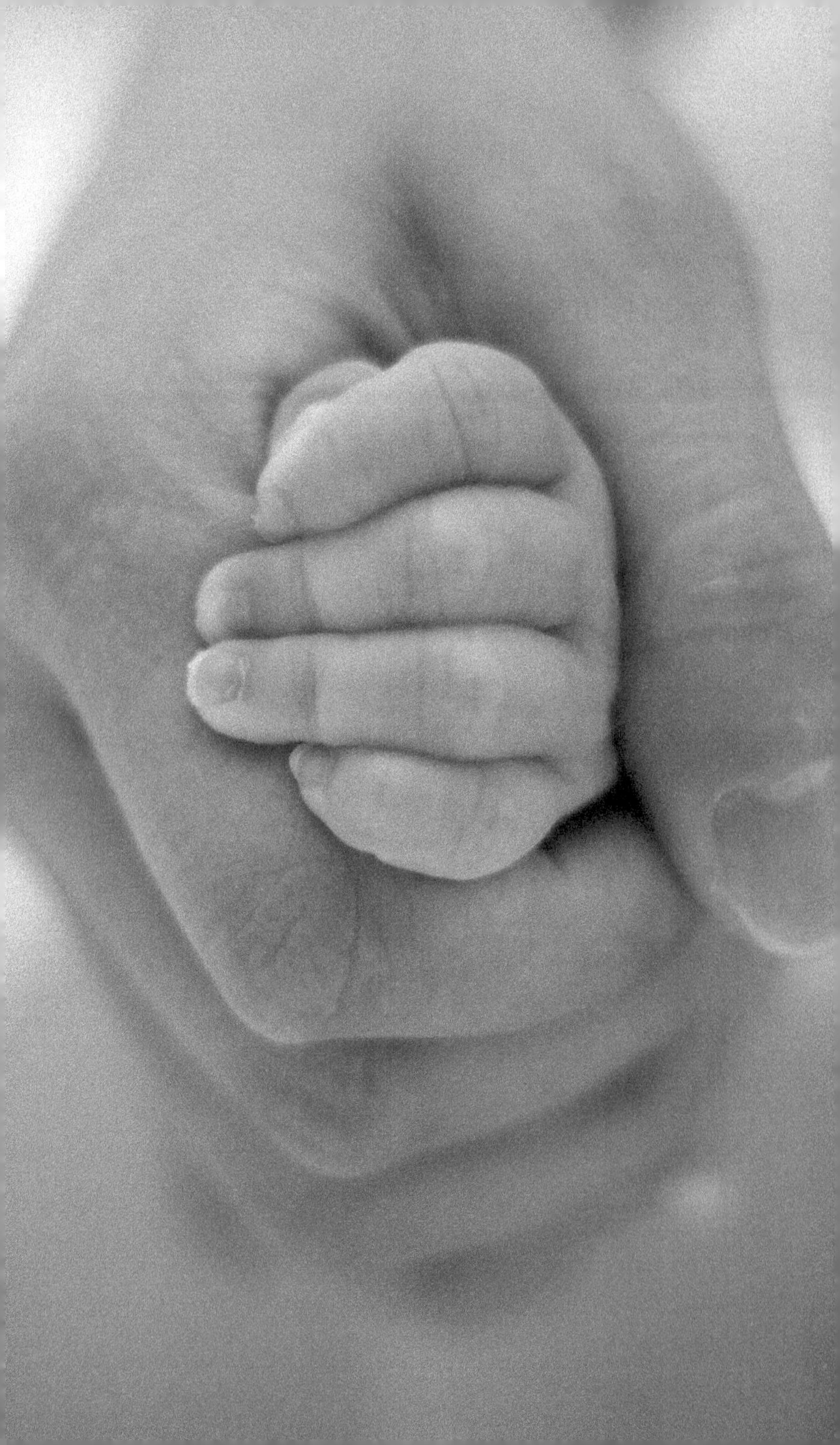

Chapter 23

Born Again

In John chapter 3 we are told the story of the secret conversation between Jesus and Nicodemus. How do we become born again?

Jesus and Nicodemus – John 3:3-8

> 3 Jesus replied, "I tell you the solemn truth, *unless a person is* ***born*** *from above, he cannot* ***see the kingdom of God***."
> 4 Nicodemus said to him, "How can a man be born when he is old? He cannot enter his mother's womb and be born a second time,

> can he?"
> 5 Jesus answered, "I tell you the solemn truth, *unless a person is **born** of **water and spirit**, he cannot enter the kingdom of God.*
> 6 What is born of the flesh is flesh, *and what is **born** of the Spirit is spirit.*
> 7 Do not be amazed that I said to you, 'You must all be born from above.'
> 8 The wind blows wherever it will, and you hear the sound it makes, but do not know where it comes from and where it is going. *So it is with everyone who is **born** of the Spirit.*"

Jesus says that we need to be born again to see the Kingdom of God. Being born again does not mean a physical rebirth, but a spiritual one. A spiritual rebirth implies that the spirit of a person who was previously dead now has come alive.

When our spirit is born again, it is the same as receiving salvation. The rebirth consists of two things, water and spirit. We are saved through a cleansing bath of the heart, and that we are renewed by the Holy Spirit.

Born of God

> [13]– *children not born by human parents or*
> *by human desire or a husband's decision,*
> ***but by God***.

— John 1:13

When we are born again, it is not through the will of any man, but it is God giving birth to us. We can not by ourselves be born again if it is not God who does it through his power.

A First Fruit

> [18] By his sovereign plan he gave us birth
> through the message of truth, that we
> would be a kind of firstfruits of all he
> created.

— James 1:18

We are a first-fruits to God when he births us again. We are born through the word of truth that sanctifies us.

Not Born by Works

> [4] But "when the kindness of God our Savior and his love for mankind appeared, [5] he saved us not by works of righteousness that we have done but on the basis of his mercy, *through the **washing** of the new **birth** and the renewing of the Holy Spirit*,
>
> — Titus 3:4-5

We have never contributed to our rebirth. It is God who has given this to us thanks to his kindness and love.

There is nothing we can add to be born again. Nothing of what we can do will ever be in our favor to be born again. Everything comes from God, through his mercy.

Believe That Jesus Is Christ

> [1] Whosoever believes that Jesus is the Christ is born of God: and every one that

> loves him that begat loves him also that is begotten of him.
>
> — 1 John 5:1 (KJV)

What characterizes that someone has been born again, is that they believe that Jesus is Christ and that they also love all the others that God has given birth to.

It would be impossible for a born-again believer not to love all the other spiritual siblings.

Born Unto a Hope

> [3] Blessed be the God and Father of our Lord Jesus Christ! By his great mercy he gave us new birth into a living hope through the resurrection of Jesus Christ from the dead,
>
> — 1 Peter 1:3

The one who has been born again, is born to new hope. It's in and through the resurrection of Jesus Christ that God has birthed us. The hope that we now have is that we will rise once from the dead to eternal life and the eternity together with God.

An Imperishable Seed

> [23] You have been born anew, not from perishable but from imperishable seed, through the living and enduring word of God.
>
> — 1 Peter 1:23

We have been born of an imperishable seed. That is so that we get preserved until the end.

Chapter 24

The Narrow Gate

> [13] "Enter through the **narrow** gate, because the gate is wide and the way is spacious that leads to destruction, and there are many who enter through it. [14] *But* ***the gate is narrow*** *and the way is difficult that leads to* ***life****, and there are few who find it.*
>
> — Matthew 7:13-14

To begin with, the Bible tells of the narrow and the wide, where the wide leads to ruin and the narrow to everlasting life. The other is a breakdown by gate and path. That is something that has a beginning and is then followed by a journey.

The gate is the beginning of something. The gateway to finding everlasting life is cramped, so it is not easy to get into it, and worse is, that few find it. Thus, we must both earnestly seek the narrow gate as well as work to get through it.

Fight to Come Through

> [24] ***Exert every effort*** *to enter through the* ***narrow door****, because many, I tell you, will try to enter and will not be able to.*
>
> — Luke 13:24

We are encouraged to fight to enter through the Narrow Gate. Do not take it lightly to get through. Do not be fooled that you're through just because someone else tells you. We need to seriously learn how to come through.

Jesus Is the Gate

> [9] I (Jesus) am the door. *If* ***anyone enters***

> ***through me***, *he will be* ***saved***, *and will come in and go out, and find pasture.*
>
> — John 10:9

It is Jesus who is the gate. No person can come through the gate in his own power or through his own merits, only by Jesus letting us through.

The gate is also the beginning of salvation. Whoever enters through Jesus is saved. Thus, they are not saved, but gets saved and hopefully completes salvation by walking on the Narrow Road.

Impossible For People

Is it possible for ordinary people to come into the Kingdom of God?

Needle's Eye - Mark 10:23-27

> 23 Then Jesus looked around and said to his disciples, "How hard it is for the rich to enter the kingdom of God!"
> 24 The disciples were astonished at these words. But again Jesus said to them,

> "Children, how hard it is to enter the kingdom of God!
> 25 *It is easier for a camel to go through the* ***eye of a needle*** *than for a rich person to enter the* ***kingdom of God***.
> 26 They were even more astonished and said to one another, "Then who can be saved?"
> 27 Jesus looked at them and replied, "*This is impossible for mere humans, but not for God; all things are* ***possible for God***."

No person can enter the Kingdom of God. The example that a camel could come through a needle eye is an image of how unrealistic it is. The problem is not that God can not do miracles, he can, and he does.

The problem lies with us, our will and ability to bow for Jesus. The reason that it would be harder for a rich man is that he has more to lose.

For God to take us through the Narrow Gate, we must be prepared to lose ourselves to God. We must put down our pride, our ambitions, surrender to God and let us be brought to repentance, by divine sorrow over sin as the Holy Spirit leads.

The only thing is, it is so hard! It is very easy for the

flesh, our sinful nature to resist. Therefore, it is on us to be really heartbroken before God and extremely serious in seeking Jesus as our savior.

Chapter 25

The Narrow (and Holy) Way

The Narrow Way

When God has taken you through the Narrow Gate, which is Jesus, you will find yourself on the road. The way is the distance that we are supposed to walk with God, after the cleansing of the heart when we received salvation. The Narrow Gate is only the beginning of salvation. The walk on the Narrow Way with God is the next part of the actual salvation work.

> [13] Enter through the narrow gate, because
> the gate is wide and the way is spacious

> that leads to destruction, and there are many who enter through it. [14] *But the gate is narrow and the* ***way*** *is difficult that* ***leads to life****, and there are few who find it.*
>
> — Matthew 7:13-14

The reason that the road is narrow; is because we have to abstain from what is in the world and keep to the grace we find in Christ.

The Original Christianity

> [26] ...Now it was in Antioch that the disciples were first called *Christians.*
>
> — Acts 11:26

What does *Christian* mean? *Christian* is a moniker for those who follow Christ, God's anointed one. Before the followers of Jesus were known as Christians, the faith was known under a different name.

At several places in the book of Acts (19:9, 23, 22:4, 24:14, 22) a different name is mentioned. The name of the faith that Jesus' disciples followed was *the Way.* Paul tells how he was a persecutor of those who followed *the Way*. Later, after Paul's conversion, he considered himself a follower of *the Way*.

Jesus Is the Way

> [4] And you know **the way** where I am going."
> [5] Thomas said, "Lord, we don't know where you are going. How can we know the way?"
> [6] Jesus replied, "*I am **the way**, and the truth, and the life*. No one comes to the Father except through me.
>
> — John 14:4-6

Jesus is the Way. We walk with him, and the goal for us is to be like him. When we walk on the Narrow Road, we transform into his likeness.

The Way is the distance we have to walk to fulfill our salvation. Without walking this distance, we suffer shipwreck in our faith when we go through tough situations in life.

The Way to Zion

The Way is not only the Narrow Path but also the way of holiness. Isaiah prophesied about this way.

The Way of Holiness – Isaiah 35:8-10, (KJV)

> 8 And an highway shall be there, and a way, and it shall be called **The way of holiness**; *the unclean shall not pass over it; but it shall be for those*: the wayfaring men, though fools, shall not err therein.
> 9 No lion shall be there, nor any ravenous beast shall go up thereon, it shall not be found there; but the redeemed shall walk there:
> 10 *And the **ransomed** of the Lord shall return, and **come to Zion** with songs* and everlasting joy upon their heads: they shall obtain joy and gladness, and sorrow and sighing shall flee away.

The way of holiness is the distance that the unclean have to walk to become holy. When we walk on that road, we become like Jesus.

A fool can not go wrong on that road because it is the Holy Spirit who leads them on the Way, he who is the helper.

Those whom Jesus has bought with his shed blood on the Cross of Calvary shall come to Zion. This means that the journey is not forever, but there is a final destination to reach.

Thus, salvation begins with the Narrow Gate, walking a distance called the way of holiness and finally reaching the destination of Zion.

The Heavenly Jerusalem

> [22] *But you have come to* **Mount Zion**, *the city of the living God, the heavenly Jerusalem*, and to myriads of angels, to the assembly [23] and congregation of the firstborn, who are enrolled in heaven, and to God, the judge of all, and to the spirits of the righteous, who have been made perfect,
>
> — Hebrews 12:22-23

Zion is the New Covenant and the New Jerusalem. The New Jerusalem is currently placed in heaven but is meant to come down to the earth at the end of this age after the final judgment.

But Zion is also a place that we can come to in this life. Zion is the place where the glory of God dwells. Those who arrive there will have access to the full inheritance of the New Covenant.

Chapter 26

Faith in Jesus

Righteous by Faith

> 16 yet we know that no one is justified by the works of the law but by the faithfulness of Jesus Christ. And we have come to believe in Christ Jesus, so that we may be **justified** by the **faithfulness** of **Christ** and not by the works of the law, because by the works of the law no one will be justified.
>
> — Galatians 2:16

There is nothing we can do to become righteous. There is no kind of good works or any amount of goodness that will save us. The only thing that can save us is that we believe in Jesus Christ. We are only justified by the faith in Jesus Christ, the Savior.

According to Your Faith

We can read in the Bible, over and over again, that Jesus always asked the people who sought to be healed whether they believed. There is a correlation between God answering us and us believing.

As You Believe – Matthew 9:27-29

> 27 As Jesus went on from there, two blind men followed him, shouting, "Have mercy on us, Son of David!"
> 28 When he went into the house, the blind men came to him. Jesus said to them, "*Do you believe that I am able to do this?*" They said to him, "*Yes, Lord.*"
> 29 Then he touched their eyes saying, "*Let it be done for you **according** to your **faith**.*"

When we believe God for something, we get it according to our faith. That is why it is so important that we believe the truth. If we do not know the truth but believe a lie, then that is what we get.

Therefore, we must believe the Gospel, as it is presented to us in the Bible. Believing in Jesus Christ also means to acknowledge the full Gospel, which includes believing in, but not limited to:

- That Jesus is God's only begotten Son
- That Jesus is God in human form
- That Jesus was sinless and never sinned
- That he died for our sins, weaknesses and diseases
- That he resurrected from the dead and defeated death

There is so much more that is part of the Gospel than what is mentioned here, but it is still the most foundational parts. May it be unto you as you believe.

Whoever Believes Shall Have Everlasting Life

> [40] For this is the will of my Father– for everyone who looks on the Son and believes in him to have eternal life, and I will raise him up at the last day."
>
> — John 6:40

It is the will of God, whoever that believes in Jesus should have eternal life and will rise on the last day. The whole Christian faith is based on, that we are destined not to perish but to live.

Partially it is about to live spiritually so that we do not remain dead and separated from God. Due the fall of humanity in the garden of Eden, we are by nature dead and lack fellowship with God.

By the end of time, everyone will rise from the dead. Those who are justified will arise to everlasting life. A life together with Jesus Christ in the New Jerusalem that is to come down from heaven and with a resurrection body similar to the shape of the angels.

Blessed Those Who Believe

> 29 Jesus said to him, "Have you believed because you have seen me? *Blessed are the people who have not seen and yet have believed.*"
>
> — John 20:29

One of the disciples of Jesus, Thomas, the doubter, could not believe that Jesus was the Savior until he had stuck his fingers through the wounds of Jesus.

The rest of the disciples believed in Jesus because they had seen him. They had lived with him for three years and witnessed him doing miracles. They had been involved in doing miracles themselves in the name of Jesus.

Blessed are those who believe in the crucifixion, death, and resurrection of Jesus, without having seen Jesus with their own eyes. Those who receive the Gospel in pure faith, even though they have not seen him.

An Opportunity For Everyone

> [31] Because he has appointed a day, in the which he will judge the world in righteousness by that man (Jesus) whom he has ordained; *whereof he has given* ***assurance*** *unto all men, in that he has* ***raised*** *him from the dead.*
>
> — Acts 17:31 (KJV)

Justification through faith is not limited to a small group of people. Faith in Jesus Christ is something that God offers to every one of us, through the death and resurrection of Jesus.

All people have a God-given opportunity to receive righteousness through faith, and that is a faith that God wants to give us. If we do not have faith, we can have it given to us, everyone included, whoever it may be.

The Promise Through Faith in Jesus

> [22] But the scripture imprisoned everything

> and everyone under sin so that **the promise** could be given– because of the **faithfulness** of Jesus Christ– to those who **believe**.
>
> — Galatians 3:22

The first covenant between God and humanity, which is the foundation for salvation, is the covenant between God and Abraham. The promise of that covenant was inherited by Isaac, and then Jacob. That promise was then carried on, through the covenant of Sinai, to the people of Israel. But this promise is not fulfilled until Jesus sealed the covenant of Zion, on the Cross of Calvary.

It is on the Cross as the Promise was fulfilled. The promise of the inheritance of everlasting life and righteousness, and all that is mentioned in the scriptures. Abraham was justified because he believed God about the Promise. In the same way, we are justified by faith in Jesus Christ, and through the covenant of Zion, we have access to the promised inheritance.

Chapter 27

Faith Comes by Hearing

Please God

> [6] Now without faith it is impossible to please him, *for the one who approaches God **must believe** that he exists and that he rewards those who seek him.*
>
> — Hebrews 11:6

There is only one way to please God, and it is to believe that he exists and rewards us for seeking him. What opens up for his mercy, is that we have faith in him. Without faith, there is no mercy. It is by his mercy and kindness that grace is available through faith.

Faith Like a Mustard Seed

> [6] So the Lord replied, "*If you had **faith** the size of a mustard seed, you could say to this black mulberry tree, 'Be pulled out by the roots and planted in the sea,' and it would **obey** you.*"
>
> — Luke 17:6

It doesn't matter what size your faith is, small or great. The importance is, that you set what faith you have to God and that it is real faith. Then God will respond through his mercy and come through to you.

God does not see to the greatness but the sincerity. If you come to God with a sincere heart, then he wants to answer you.

Saving Faith

> [5] *so that your faith would not be based on*

> *human wisdom but on the **power of God**.*
>
> — 1 Corinthians 2:5

There is a difference between believing and having faith. Most people who believe something, often have an intellectual or emotional belief, which implies that the faith in God is based on a logical conclusion or an emotional state.

The faith that touches God is the faith that comes from the inner of the heart, that believes that God is personal and that he is interested in us. He is a personal God that we can know and trust, just like a close friend.

Faith Comes From Hearing

> 17 Consequently **faith** comes from what is
> **heard**, and what is heard comes through
> the **preached** word of Christ.
>
> — Romans 10:17

If I don't have faith, where then can I get it? The Bible says that faith comes by hearing, specifically the hearing of the preached word of Christ. Those who are acquainted with the scriptures knows that Jesus is referred to as the living *Word of God*.

When we study the scriptures and learn to know the truth of God, that truth will set us free. That means that when the truth is spoken, faith comes into our hearts and becomes active.

> [2] and by which you are being saved, *if you* ***hold firmly*** *to the* ***message*** *I preached to you*– unless you believed in vain.
>
> — 1 Corinthians 15:2

The Gospel is the message of joy, the story of Jesus and the salvation for us. If we believe the Gospel and hold on to it, we will eventually be saved.

A Faith That Grows

> [3] We are bound to thank God always for you, brothers, as it is meet, *because that your* ***faith grows*** *exceedingly, and the charity of every one of you all toward each other abounds;*
>
> — 2 Thessalonians 1:3 (KJV)

If we have a small amount of faith, with which we received Jesus. That faith may grow by seeking God, praying and doing what is right towards our neighbor. Then our faith will increase as we walk with Jesus and become more like him.

Chapter 28

The Cross

Jesus Humbled on the Cross

Philippians 2:6-8

> 6 who though he existed in the form of God did not regard equality with God as something to be grasped,
> 7 but emptied himself by taking on the form of a slave, by looking like other men, and by sharing in human nature.

> 8 He humbled himself, by becoming obedient
> to the point of death– even death on a cross!

Jesus is entirely God and fully human. He came to earth to show us the Way. This was an incredible step, from sitting on the right side of the father in heaven, to be born in a mortal human body.

Then he became the servant of all humanity, he was mocked by the Pharisees and humiliated in every way possible.

In the end, he was obedient to God the Father; he died on the Cross of Calvary for the sins of all the world. Executed by the cruelest method known to humanity for maximum suffering. After being whipped, beaten and tortured, made a spectacle for all of Jerusalem to see. Jesus chose to do it for the Father's love of humanity, and for you and me.

The Cross - the Power of God

> 18 For the message about **the cross is**
> **foolishness** to those who are perishing,

> but to us who are being saved it is the
> **power of God**.
>
> — 1 Corinthians 1:18

For those that are strong in themselves and prideful, Jesus' death on the Cross appears like foolishness. Why did Jesus have to die, why not just beat the crap out of the devil?

But for those who have insight into their weakness and have experienced what God has done for them, it is a power unto salvation. All this to humble the prideful ones!

Our Sins Crucified With Jesus

> 24 *He himself* ***bore our sins*** *in his body on the tree, that we may cease from sinning and* ***live for righteousness***. By his wounds you were healed.
>
> — 1 Peter 2:24

The crucifixion was a sin offering for the sins of the

world. Through the shedding of his blood, he has washed us clean so that we can receive justification as a gift. Without the righteousness of God, we can not approach God.

Our Debt Crucified With Jesus

> 13 And even though you were dead in your transgressions and in the uncircumcision of your flesh, he nevertheless made you alive with him, having forgiven all your transgressions. 14 *He has destroyed what was against us, a certificate of* ***indebtedness*** *expressed in decrees opposed to us. He has taken it away by* ***nailing it to the cross***.
>
> — Colossians 2:13-14

The crucifixion was also a guilt offering, with which Jesus paid the price for the debt we incurred through our transgressions. The debt certificate has been nailed to the Cross of Calvary, and therefore God does not require revenge on us when we receive salvation.

Jesus' Victory on the Cross

> 15 *Disarming the rulers and authorities, he has made a public disgrace of them,* ***triumphing*** *over them* ***by the cross****.*
>
> — Colossians 2:15

The crucifixion may look like a defeat at first because Jesus had to die. But what Jesus did for real was to defeat Satan's powers. When God forgave the sins on the Cross, there was no longer anything to accuse us of; thereby the devil lost his strength against those who have received Jesus.

In the days of the Roman Empire, the field marshals used to celebrate triumph when they had won a victory over another kingdom or empire. Prisoners of war had to parade naked through the streets of Rome to become a public spectacle. This has Jesus done with all fallen angels and demons before all the hosts of heaven.

LEGAL

Chapter 29

Justification

In his letter to the Romans, Paul describes in chapter 4 how we can be declared righteous, that is justified. Not by our strength, but by grace.

Declared Righteous – Romans 4:2-8

> [2] For if Abraham was declared righteous by
> the works of the law, he has something to
> boast about– but not before God.
> [3] For what does the scripture say? "Abraham
> believed God, and it was credited to him as
> righteousness."

> [4] Now to the one who works, his pay is not credited due to grace but due to obligation.
> [5] But to the one who does not work, but believes in the one who declares the ungodly righteous, his faith is credited as righteousness.
> [6] So even David himself speaks regarding the blessedness of the man to whom God credits righteousness apart from works:
> [7] "Blessed are those whose lawless deeds are forgiven, and whose sins are covered;
> [8] blessed is the one against whom the Lord will never count sin."

Righteousness is something we lacked by ourselves when we once were the children of the world. Those who have received Jesus as Lord and has been saved has received a righteousness that is from God.

No Justification Through the Law

> [21] But now apart from the law the righteousness of God (which is attested by the law and the prophets) has been

> disclosed– [22] *namely, the righteousness of God through the faithfulness of Jesus Christ* ***for all who believe****. For there is no distinction,*
>
> — Romans 3:21-22

The mosaic law tells how a person has to live to be seen as righteous. The problem is that no one becomes righteous by keeping the Law. The Law only reveals our sins and transgressions and exposes how miserable we are.

Throughout history, the people of Israel have sought to gain righteousness and have tried to find it by the Law, by their own accomplishments.

But since the Law cannot save anyone, no one has ever received justice by keeping it.

Abraham Justified by Faith

> [6] *And he believed in the Lord; and he* ***counted*** *it to him for* ***righteousness****.*
>
> — Genesis 15:6 (KJV)

Abraham, the forefather to the people of Israel, never won righteousness by keeping any laws. Similarly, there was neither law to keep for Abraham to gain righteousness.

What Abraham did was to believe God for the promise that he had been given, and through the faith in God, he was justified. Abraham received his righteousness from God as a gift.

> [6] *Blessed are those who hunger and thirst for* ***righteousness****, for they will be* ***satisfied****.*
>
> — Matthew 5:6

God has promised that all who hunger and thirst for righteousness shall be satisfied. God turns to all those who long and seek for him.

Justified by Faith in the Gospel

> [17] For the righteousness of God is revealed in the gospel from faith to faith, just as it is written, "The righteous by faith will live."
>
> — Romans 1:17

If you have received Jesus as Lord in your life and have been saved, believe in Jesus' crucifixion, death, and resurrection. Then you have become justified as a gift from God. You are not righteous by yourself, and you do not deserve that, but by faith, you have received it as a gift.

> [30] What shall we say then?– that the Gentiles who did not pursue righteousness obtained it, that is, a righteousness that is by faith,
>
> — Romans 9:30

The Gentiles, we that are not of Jewish descent have also been given the opportunity to be justified by faith.

Chapter 30

Reconciliation With God

The World Reconciled

> [19] For God was pleased to have all his fullness dwell in the Son [20] *and through him to* ***reconcile*** *all things to himself by* ***making peace*** *through the* ***blood of his cross****– through him, whether things on earth or things in heaven.*
>
> — Colossians 1:19-20

The world is by its very nature an enemy of everything that can be associated with God, and what comes from him. Likewise, God was also enemy of the world and its inhabitants.

The world has been reconciled with God, through the blood of Jesus on the Cross of Calvary. It doesn't matter that the world is still hostile to God. God has reconciled the world with himself, and therefore there is peace on earth and in heaven.

Mankind Reconciled

> [21] And you were at one time strangers and enemies in your minds as expressed through your evil deeds, [22] *but now he has* ***reconciled*** *you by his physical body* ***through death*** *to present you holy, without blemish, and* ***blameless before him***–
>
> — Colossians 1:21-22

Humanity was also in enmity against God, in anticipation of judgment against those who have sinned. We were hostile toward God in our minds and actions and failed because of original sin, to not be opposed against God.

By letting Jesus suffer death on the Cross, God created peace between himself and humanity, and can, therefore, offer us repentance and salvation.

Jesus is the Mediator

> [24] For Christ did not enter a sanctuary made with hands– the representation of the true sanctuary– but into heaven itself, and he appears now in God's presence for us.
>
> — Hebrews 9:24

Jesus is our high priest and mediator. He walked before the throne of God and brought reconciliation for us before God.

He did not enter the earthly temple, but faced the altar of the heavenly tabernacle, and offered his blood as the atonement for the transgressions of the world and humanity.

Peace With God

> [1] Therefore, since we have been declared righteous by faith, we have peace with God through our Lord Jesus Christ,
>
> — Romans 5:1

If you have received Jesus as savior and become justified, then you have personally gained peace with God through faith in Jesus' crucifixion, death, and resurrection.

Boldly Before God

> [19] Having therefore, brothers, boldness to enter into the holiest by the blood of Jesus,
> [20] By a new and living way, which he has consecrated for us, through the veil, that is to say, his flesh;
>
> — Hebrews 10:19-20 (KJV)

If you have been reconciled with God, then you can walk into the most holy. The most holy represents a place in your walk with God where he is intimate.

God has opened the veil, which hindered us from a personal relationship with him, and now the way is open to those who are justified by faith.

Chapter 31

Pure Conscience and Heart

Those who are saved through faith in Jesus has also been washed clean by him. The declaration of righteousness also implies that we have become cleansed from our old dirt, the sin.

Wash Each-other's Feet - John 13:8-10

> 8 Peter said to him, "You will never wash my feet!" Jesus replied, "*If I do not **wash** you, **you have no share with me**.*"
> 9 Simon Peter said to him, "Lord, wash not only my feet, but also my hands and my

> head!"
> [10] Jesus replied, "*The one who has **bathed** needs only to wash his feet*, but is completely clean. And you disciples are clean, but not every one of you."

It is necessary that we have been washed white, to have a part in Christ.

Born Again Through a Bath

> [5] he saved us not by works of righteousness that we have done but on the basis of his mercy, through the **washing** of the **new birth** and the **renewing** of the Holy Spirit,
>
> — Titus 3:5

When you received Jesus in your heart when God brought you through the Narrow Gate, you were bathed, that implies that you were born again.

To be born again, and have a cleansing bath of the heart goes hand in hand. The purification bath means that you are renewed through the Holy Spirit.

Washed Clean

> [11] Some of you once lived this way. But you were **washed**, you were sanctified, you were justified in the name of the Lord Jesus Christ and by the Spirit of our God.
>
> — 1 Corinthians 6:11

Being washed clean implies that we have become justified. The justification and the purifying bath are connected, and all this through the name of Jesus Christ and the Spirit of God.

A Pure Conscience - Hebrews 9:13-14

> [13] For if the blood of goats and bulls and the ashes of a young cow sprinkled on those who are defiled consecrated them and provided ritual purity,
> [14] how much more will the **blood of Christ**, who through the eternal Spirit offered himself without blemish to God, **purify our consciences** from dead works to worship the living God.

How do you know that you have been justified and have become born again? The big sign is the inward sanitation bath, where the conscience and the heart are washed clean. When Jesus had washed you clean, you notice it. Then you get peace in your mind; you also see that your thoughts are different.

The dirty heart thinks of evil, money, itself, violence, anger and much more. When the heart and conscience have become clean, then there will be a discernible difference in your mind, when the thoughts of Christ dwells there instead. The difference is distinct, like day and night.

Bold Before God

> [22] let us draw near with a sincere heart in the assurance that faith brings, because we have had our **hearts** sprinkled **clean** from an **evil conscience** and our bodies washed in pure water.
>
> — Hebrews 10:22

When our conscience is no longer evil, and the heart is clean, we can boldly come before God, because we are his children.

Confession Through Baptism

> [21] And this prefigured baptism, which now saves you– not the washing off of physical dirt but the *pledge of a **good conscience** to God– through the resurrection of Jesus Christ,*
>
> — 1 Peter 3:21

Once we have become cleansed inside, we are invited to proclaim it on the outside. Baptism in water is the outwardly ritual of proclamation that expresses the pledge of a pure conscience. The baptism should never take place without a true inner cleansing; otherwise, it's just dead works.

Wash Each-other's Feet

> [13] You call me "Teacher" and "Lord", and do so correctly, for that is what I am. [14] If I then, your Lord and Teacher, have **washed**

> your feet, you too **ought** to **wash** one **another's feet**.
>
> — John 13:13-14

The parable when Jesus is washing the disciples' feet, is a symbolic act of God forgiving us of our sins. To wash the whole body is a symbol of regeneration.

The necessity of having our feet washed, is a symbol that we need to confess our sins on a regular basis. Because we live in the world, we soil our feet again and therefore still needs forgiveness from God.

Jesus urges us to wash each other's feet, which means we will have to forgive each other the sins others do unto us. Otherwise, it will be hard for us to keep up with Jesus and we start to fall behind.

Conclusion

Salvation Prayer!?

What is the salvation prayer? Within the evangelical movement it is known as the prayer you are supposed to get the convert to say to become saved.

Now, this theology or church tradition is very flawed. I have not been able to find any places in the Bible that support the idea, that a particular prayer would get you saved.

There are already formulated prayers in the Bible, for example, "Our father." Also, the book of Psalms is full of written down prayers. But there is no such thing as saying a magic prayer and things will happen automagically.

> [6] Now without faith it is impossible to please him, for the one who approaches God must believe that he exists and that he rewards those who seek him.
>
> — Hebrews 11:6

If you have read through this book and understood the teachings in each chapter, you should realize by now, that it is the state of your heart that is important whether God will answer your prayers. It has to come from the heart!

The purpose of this book has been, to try to affect your heart in the direction where your heart needs to be, to be prepared to receive Jesus as your Lord.

You can if you want, pray a prayer of submitting your heart in the hands of God. That is the choice of your free will. Maybe your heart is ready, and God will take you through the Narrow Gate. Perhaps it's not ready yet, even if you want to follow God. You can still say a prayer expressing your willingness to become his child.

> [4] Or do you have contempt for the wealth

> of his kindness, forbearance, and patience,
> and yet do not know that God's kindness
> leads you to repentance?
>
> — Romans 2:4

Maybe God still has to work more on your heart. Don't be worried; he has the will and the wisdom, to lead you to the right place, where you are ready to receive him in your heart.

In fact, there is a salvation prayer in the Bible. That is Psalm 51. This psalm was written by King David when he had murdered Uriah, to cover up his adultery with his wife.

> 19 My sacrifice to God is a broken spirit;
> God, you won't spurn a broken, chastened
> heart.
>
> — Psalm 51:19 (CJB)

In that psalm David pour out his heart before God. The psalm reflects the state of David's heart when it is in the state, to have a godly sorrow over his sin. It is recommended that you read and study this psalm, and try to understand it. Ask God to put your heart in the same state over your sin.

Realize that you have sinned, but also that you have sinned against God and grieved him. When the day and time comes that your heart is in the right state, God will do the miracle of birthing you again, and put you on the Narrow Path of holiness leading to God's holy city.

www.ingramcontent.com/pod-product-compliance
Lightning Source LLC
Chambersburg PA
CBHW060236050426
42448CB00009B/1469

* 9 7 8 9 1 9 8 4 7 5 2 3 4 *